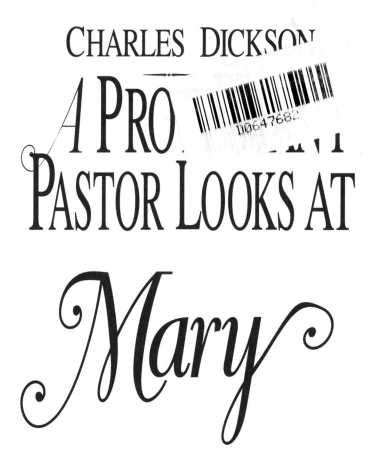

CHARLES DICKSON

A PROTESTANT
PASTOR LOOKS AT

Mary

Our Sunday Visitor Publishing Division
Our Sunday Visitor, Inc.
Huntington, Indiana 46750

Cover design by Monica Watts

TABLE OF CONTENTS

Foreword

As the Christian faith moves forward to the beginning of the third millennium, we stand on the brink of one of the most exciting breakthroughs in our history. Traditional misunderstandings and barriers of the past are slowly giving way to the new breath of fresh air that is beginning to dominate our thinking.

Ecumenical relations are at their highest point in the five centuries that have elapsed since the tragic split in the Western Church. One of the foremost topics under discussion is the place of the Virgin Mary in Christian thought and practice. Perhaps it may be considered unusual if not even strange that a Lutheran clergyman should write on what is generally regarded as a "Catholic" topic. Yet it seems the time has arrived for such a publication that is neither polemical nor patronizing but (in a hopefully objective manner) considers Mariology in its scriptural, liturgical, ecclesiological, and doctrinal development.

Perhaps the following pages will be sufficiently controversial — or at least thought-provoking — to promote discussion and sufficiently sensitive to promote new understandings.

If both of these things occur as a result of these writings, I will have accomplished my purpose of building another span across the gap of misunderstanding and — like the Blessed Virgin herself — a bridge to ultimate Christian unity.

Setting the Stage

In order to understand any phenomenon existing in the present, we must attempt to gain some knowledge of its past. What is true of other concerns in the Church is no less true of Mariology. This section deals with the background of thought concerning Mary, the manner in which the Christian community sought to honor her, the thinking of those who opposed such devotional practices, the emergence of official doctrine regarding her position in salvation history, and the possibility of altered Protestant approaches to the whole field of Mariology.

It is on this latter note that we begin as we look at a heretofore unheard-of scenario in the first two chapters — a Protestant Mariology. Will it happen? What needs to take place if it does? What forces are holding it back? And, what are its possible contributions to the ecumenical movement?

1

❦ ❄ ❧

Is a Protestant Mariology Possible?

The history of Christianity in the past two decades has been, to no small degree, a history of reconsiderations. Viewpoints and practices once firmly entrenched are now being challenged, and forms of expression that were either neglected or rejected are now being reexamined. One need only to cite the new concern for effective preaching among Roman Catholics, the new emphasis on the sacraments among Protestants, a sociopolitical dimension among fundamentalists, and experimentation with free worship experiences among the traditional liturgical churches as illustrative of this phenomenon. Reconsideration seems to be a recurring theme among all Christian groups, yet only time will reveal the depth or longevity of such movements.

Amidst these changes lies a dormant theme only lightly touched upon for the past five centuries, that is, the place of the Virgin Mary in Protestant theology and practice. A recent booklet emerging from the Catholic-Lutheran dialogue, which is entitled *Mary in Evangelical Perspective*, attempts to deal with the subject, but the question remains: Is a Protestant Mariology possible — or for that matter, necessary?

Two decades ago, in his essay on the topic of

Mariology, Edmund Schlick viewed the Roman Catholic position on Mary in the midst of efforts for closer relations between the churches as "a fundamental veto on the part of the Roman Church." A few years later, Jaroslav Pelikan, in his prize-winning book, *The Riddle of Roman Catholicism*, asserted, "There is little sympathy for Mariology outside the borders of the Roman Communion." These and other statements of kindred spirit were indicative of two problems, the first being an apparent lack of awareness of the definite Mariology among millions of the world's Eastern Orthodox plus the significant Anglo-Catholic commitment within Anglicanism. The second and perhaps even more important problem than this oversight was the fact that they tended to reinforce the five-century-old barrier at least partially created and certainly perpetuated by the very mention of the topic.

Of course the realization that some seventy percent of world Christendom accords a significant position of the Virgin Mary in its theology should not, in itself, be grounds for a Protestant reconsideration, since theology is not supposed to be constructed by statistical surveys. Yet, this realization is one in which Protestants may be ill-advised to ignore, given the thesis that theology emerges from the corporate experience of peoples and cultures.

If not from a statistical basis, can there emerge a Protestant Mariology on the basis of theology itself? Jesuit theologian Yves M. J. Congar believes there is a fundamental difference between the groups due to Protestantism's disregard of what he terms, "the role of humanity in salvation." In emphasizing the divine nature of Christ, Father Congar feels Protestant theology has all but ignored the human nature, thus explaining a strong emphasis in preaching upon the Atonement but little on the Incarnation. In support of this he cites both Martin Luther and Karl Barth, who assumed a wide gap between the two natures of Christ, attributing the work of salvation to the divine alone and emptying of value the human action of the Word made flesh.

In 451 the Council of Chalcedon dealt with the subject of dual natures by affirming the inseparability of the two natures, each nature being preserved and concurring in one person (*prosopon*) and one subsistence (*hypostasis*). If this Chalcedonian formulation is given serious attention in contemporary Protestant thought, some feel the human nature of Christ will not continue to suffer the devaluation of the past nor will therefore its precursor in the Incarnation — the Virgin Mary.

Still another avenue to be explored in attempting to answer the question of whether or not a Protestant Mariology is possible is the psychological. Have Protestant systematics, in slighting the place of Mary in the Incarnation, produced a religious experience with a harsh masculine emphasis? Russian Orthodox theologian Nicolay Berdyayev suggests that such an emphasis does exist and needs to be tempered by the introduction of feminine qualities. A description of the effect of such tempering is contained in Karl Adam's work *The Spirit of Catholicism* when he calls it "a gracious relation of certain ineffable and ultimate traits in the nature of God, which are too fine and too delicate to be grasped otherwise than as reflected in the mirror of a mother."

I consider the following so important that I have repeated it (with some rewording) in at least two other chapters of this work.

Some psychologists of religion suggest that Mariology makes the same psychological sense to the worshiping community of believers as allowing the boy child to engage in some playing with dolls. In each case, the rugged masculine qualities are mixed with the qualities of tenderness and affection. Could the development of a Protestant Mariology do much to temper the harsh portrayal of a God of judgment and provide it with a deeper concept of a God of mercy?

There remains at least one more avenue to be explored: the religion and science relationship. Pelikan admits that the insight of Roman Catholicism into Mariology has enabled it to "incorporate a full-blown view of the world of nature into its system without sacrificing the sovereign otherness of God."

The battles of the nineteenth and twentieth centuries between science and Protestantism certainly involved the problem of how to talk about God's being above and before the world and yet in the world amidst the processes of nature. Some historians suggest that without a mature Mariology, Protestantism has been caught in the dilemma of either stressing such involvement too directly, which diluted its concept of God to mere process, or emphasizing the lordship and otherness of the Creator to the point of abstracting Him from the natural processes.

Such a dilemma, Catholic theologians believe, can be resolved by an understanding of the Mother of God (or, in Greek, "Theotokos") as the means by which Christ became truly man involved in nature; yet he remains truly God, sovereign over nature. G. K. Chesterton stated the case in his work on St. Francis by observing that "man has stripped from his soul the last rag of nature worship and can return to nature." Can such an apparent synthesis point the way toward avoidance of the continuing strife between advancing science and rigid biblicism?

Given the interplay of world statistics, theology, psychology, and science and the role each plays in affecting the world ecumenical scene, we may well be at a point where a long-dormant subject now begins to blossom. Will it result in some kind of compromise between two ends of a spectrum, one with, at times, excessive veneration and the other with, on occasion, excessive neglect?

Perhaps a partial answer lies in the realization that ecumenical bridges are constructed by people with a passion for dialogue in the same manner as the tempo of a game is determined by the nature of its players. Whether a Protestant Mariology emerges on the world ecumenical stage may, in the final analysis, depend upon the players.

Discussion Questions

1. What changes do you see taking place in your community that indicate better understanding between Catholics and Protestants?

2. Do you feel there is an element of tenderness in Catholic religious practice that is missing in Protestant worship? Can this be attributed to the importance given to Mary?

3. Does emphasis on the Virgin and her place in history make the idea of God's mercy more real to people in general?

4. Find out what you can about the position of the Catholic Church on science and religion.

5. Are you aware of examples of what you would call "excessive veneration" of Mary in Catholic parishes of your community?

2

❧ ✂ ❧

A Protestant Looks at Mary

Of all the issues that have divided Christians for the past five centuries, few have received more attention than has the subject of the Virgin Mary. Protestants accuse Catholics of engaging in undue veneration that is beyond the intent of the Scriptures, and Catholics retaliate by accusing Protestants of ignoring the position that is rightfully hers as the Mother of our Lord. The truth may lie somewhere in between the two accusations.

Traditionally, Protestant leaders have felt the attention accorded Mary in Catholic theology and worship has constituted a major stumbling block to the establishment of closer relations between the churches.

On the other hand, Catholics feel that Protestants have ignored the place of Mary in history and thereby stripped her of the honor that should be given to the one woman in history whom God chose to be the Mother of His Son. The struggle to bridge the gap between these two opposing views has been both long and intense. To understand its development in Christian experience and history we must begin with. . .

THE BIBLICAL BACKGROUND ◆ Scriptural allusions to the place of Mary in history are recorded in the Old Testament book of Genesis (3:15) and in the prophet Isaiah (7:14) among others, but Mary enters the stage of history in the New Testament Gospels of St. Matthew and St. Luke as the maiden betrothed to Joseph. The archangel Gabriel announces that she is to be the Mother of God's Son. Shortly thereafter, Elizabeth (who is to become the mother of John) salutes Mary and her unique position in history. When Joseph learns of Mary's pregnancy, he makes plans to divorce her on the assumption she has committed adultery but is informed that her conception is of the Holy Spirit. He takes her as his wife, and they journey to Bethlehem to be enrolled for tax purposes. During this time she gives birth to the Christ Child and then they are warned in a dream to flee to Egypt to avoid the wrath of Herod. In about a year they return to Nazareth where the boy Jesus grows up working with His father.

Once our Lord's ministry begins, Mary is mentioned on four more occasions: (1) at the marriage at Cana, (2) at a gathering in Capernaum, (3) at the Crucifixion, and (4) after the Ascension.

With the close of the biblical canon, the period of Church history and tradition becomes the source for Christian teaching and practice. During the early years, the Apostles', Nicene, and Athanasian Creeds were developed. These statements of belief are accepted by the majority of the world's Christians and included in many of their worship services. While not being stated explicitly in the Scriptures, the creeds are statements of the main teachings of Scripture.

Much else has developed from Christian tradition as well, among them the various forms of

Church organizational structures and forms of worship. Included in this tradition has been the development of beliefs concerning the place of the Virgin Mary in salvation history. It is at this juncture that Catholic and Protestant viewpoints begin to pursue separate paths. One Lutheran theologian stated, "There is probably no place where the difference between the two understandings of Christianity become so plain as in their differing conceptions of the Virgin Mary." This, then, leads us to a look at. . .

THE FUNDAMENTAL PROBLEMS ◆ These problems seem to merge in the doctrines of the Mother of Christ and the questions arising from them, which appear to be threefold involving the areas of (1) Scripture, (2) authority, and (3) grace.

Both Catholics and Protestants recognize that our knowledge of revelation must be found within the Scriptures. Lutherans point out that dogmas such as the Assumption (celebrated on August 15) and the Immaculate Conception (December 8) are not apparent in Scripture. Catholics, on the other hand, speak of the contextual sufficiency of the Scriptures and point out that the Scriptures themselves represent theological interpretations of the community and that there can be no creation or interpretation of the Scriptures apart from the living community, which is the Church. Historians recognize the Church came before the New Testament and it is the Church that actually decided which documents should be included in the Bible, a task that was not completed until near the end of the fourth century.

On the question of authority, Luther feared that strong ecclesiastical authority can fashion belief in dogmas independent of the Scriptures while Catholics point out that since the Second Vatican Council the bishops and pope are involved in the wider context of the Church. Devotion to Mary is widespread and ancient, as is belief in her role in salvation history.

On the subject of grace, the Annunciation can be seen as an absolutely fundamental place where God's initiative and man's free will meet. Catholic theology teaches that Mary is actively, although subordinately, involved in the work of salvation.

Penetrating the above issues is the struggle to maintain in Christian thinking a balance between the human and divine natures of Christ, between the Incarnation and the Atonement, and between a God who is above and before the world and a God who continues to participate in its processes. In all these issues, the Virgin Mary is a subject of prime importance. This brings us to the point of needing to retrace the issues from. . .

THE HISTORICAL BACKGROUND ◆ Devotion to Mary developed very early in the Christian community, and early manuscripts speak of the existence of philomarian groups within the Church. The Mother of God (or Theotokos) concept was formally introduced into Church discussion at the Council of Ephesus in 431, although the term and its supporters had been part of the Christian community long before that date. It was upheld again at the Council of Chalcedon in 451. By the end of the fifth century, Marian devotion had spread and led to the incorporation of Marian feasts into the liturgical calendar, and the concept of the Immaculate Conception continued to gain momentum to the point of being widely accepted by the eve of the Reformation in the fifteenth.

Mariology was certainly not a side issue with the reformers. Luther referred to Mary as "the workshop of God," and believed that praise for her should not be based on the qualities of Mary herself but on the grace granted to her. Zwingli defended the use of Ave Maria as a means of praise to Mary stating, "The more honor and love for Christ, the more also the estcem and honor for Mary." Calvin warned of the danger of honoring her as a person rather than as the elected instrument of God but affirms, "We cannot celebrate the blessings given us in Christ without commemorating at the same time how high an honor God has granted to Mary when He chose to make her the Mother of His only Son."

The reformers and those following in their footsteps gradually became polarized in their positions. This feeling is evident in a statement made by Luther later in his life: "I could wish that the cult of Mary would be completely abrogated, solely because of abuse." From this and other statements it was obvious he felt devotion to Mary had become excessive.

In 1854 the Immaculate Conception became a dogma and in 1950 the Assumption of the Virgin Mary achieved the same status. While both of these actions tended to reflect the flow of Catholic belief and practice, they also served to widen the gap separating Protestant and Catholic traditions.

With the advent of Vatican II and an ensuing series of various Protestant-Catholic dialogues, a new age had dawned in relationships between churches. Leaders of both are now able to go beyond the previous centuries of controversies and debating points to focus in on the crucial problems that remain and that represent the different theological stances, all of which sets the stage for a look at. . .

THE STRUGGLE FOR UNDERSTANDING ◆ It cannot be ignored that Mariology in the Catholic and Orthodox traditions constitutes two-thirds of world Christendom, which creates a challenge that has to be answered by every new generation of children of the Reformation. Open-minded Christians of the Protestant tradition must ask themselves if it is reasonable to believe that throughout centuries of Christian history, two-thirds of the faithful have been misled by false doctrines and practices concerning the Mother of our Lord. To believe that such widespread grave errors existed may indeed stretch the limits of both logic and charity.

One Lutheran leader reminds us, "It is immature to say that everything we dislike in the history of Christianity is due to some outside influence, while what we approve of is the work of the Holy Spirit."

The Reformers wanted to safeguard the true measure of honor due to Mary because of the close connection with a true understanding of the work of Jesus Christ. But they did not want to see her elevated to a position they regarded as beyond the intentions of the Scriptures. Since that time and certainly to a much greater degree in our own time, both Catholic and Protestant leaders have been searching for a middle road between a Mary-less Christianity on the one side and a Marian cult on the other. From such struggles has developed the fertile soil in which shall grow. . .

THE FUTURE DIALOGUE ◆ Any attempt at reaching a consensus of belief must begin with common ground shared by all groups, and that ground seems to be the Scriptures. In Holy Writ, Christians see Mary portrayed as a woman of faith and humility that exhibit themselves in her immediate surrender of herself to the divine will, her energy and earnestness in her journey from Nazareth, the happy thanksgiving in her song, her silent, musing thoughtfulness, her pondering over the shepherds' visit, and her keeping of her Son's words in her heart. She is portrayed in Scripture as the most tender, faithful, humble, patient, and loving of women.

From the common ground of Scripture we proceed to a watermark of Church history, the Council of Chalcedon in 451, which asserted the inseparability of the natures of Christ, divine and human, as concurring in the same person. Most Protestants have tended to emphasize only the divine nature, thereby devaluating the human side, and therefore the precursor of the humanity of Christ — the Virgin Mary. The reformers assumed a wide gap between the two natures of Christ, attributing the work of salvation to the divine alone and thereby emptying of value the human action of the Word made flesh. In the process, the worship emphasis naturally followed by underlining the Atonement with relatively little attention given to the Incarnation. Part of the future of dialogue lies in achieving an understanding of the importance of both.

We recognize that Protestants for the most part must also consider the psychological impact of slighting the Virgin Mary and her place in the Incarnation. Protestantism, in general, has produced a religious experience with harsh masculine emphasis. Such harshness has been tempered in Catholic experience by the presence of feminine qualities associated with Mary. For Protestants, part of the future of dialogue lies in the attention given to the tenderness element of faith represented by Mary.

In the arena of the sciences, traditional Protestantism has often found itself involved in conflicts of creationism versus evolutionism. Catholics believe that their mature Mariology — which emphasizes a God who is above and before the world, yet involved in nature — has helped them to avoid involvement in such controversies. Without emphasis on the Incarnation, Protestants have perhaps been caught in the dilemma of either stressing the divine involvement too directly, which dilutes a concept of God to mere process, or emphasizing the lordship and otherness of God to the point of abstracting Him from the natural processes. The Incarnation and the role of Mary thus become points of discussion in future dialogue as we grapple with science and faith.

In the final analysis, Catholic and Protestant efforts toward finding a real solution must deal with both Scripture and Tradition, recognizing that each has played an important role in the development of the teachings and practices of all Christian groups. The churches must deal with the reality that revelation did not stop with the closing of the canon and that the Holy Spirit is continually active in the living community of the faithful.

The future of dialogue is the future of hope in Church relations. Such hope grows from the fertile soil of an ongoing search for a position on the Mother of God. A position that produces neither a Mary-less religion on the one hand nor a Marian cult on the other. Progress is being made, not toward reaching one solution at the expense of the other, but toward discovering the best of both.

Discussion Questions

1. Are you aware of any increasing attention being given by Protestants to the importance of Mary?

2. Why is Tradition important as well as Scriptures in helping us understand Mary's place in Christian history?

3. Find out what you can about the manner in which the Bible was finally compiled by Church leaders.

4. Do you feel that the concerns of the reformers about undue veneration of Mary were justified?

5. Is there a reasonable middle ground between excessive veneration of Mary on the one hand and neglect of her on the other?

3

♌ ✹ ♌

The Church Fathers and Mary

The subject of the place of Mary in Christian history and tradition has been one of increasing focus in modern ecumenical discussions between Catholics and various Protestant denominations. Usually such discussions have focused on ways of interpreting the biblical records and their implications for faith and practice in today's Church. One area that has been generally neglected in such dialogue is the contribution the early Church Fathers made to our understanding of Mary in the Christian faith.

During the patristic period, discussion about Mary revolved around the central issue of her relation to Jesus and His role in the plan of salvation. Jesus' birth from Mary pointed to His humanity, while the virgin conception was seen as indicative of a more than human reality in His life and work.

The earliest writings on the subject can be traced to St. Justin Martyr and St. Irenaeus, both of whom spoke of the parallelism between Eve and Mary as negative and positive aspects of the human race. They built on the imagery of the old and the new Adam already found in St. Paul and thereby initiated what many Church historians believe to be the beginnings of Marian theology. In the development of Christology an important milestone would later be reached with the definition of Mary as the

Theotokos (Mother of God) as articulated by the Council of Ephesus in 431.

One of the earliest Church Fathers to address the subject was St. Ignatius of Antioch, between 100 and 107, as part of his concern over the heresy of Docetism, which taught that Jesus was not true man but only appeared in human form. As part of his defense Ignatius stressed the birth of Jesus from a woman. Perhaps the greatest of the early apologists was Justin, who died a martyr in 165.

One of Justin's works, *Dialogue with Trypho the Jew*, was concerned to a great extent with differing views about the interpretation of the Jewish Scriptures, particularly the Immanuel passage in Isaiah 7:14. But Justin's work contains as well the seed of several important later developments, one of which is the Eve/Mary parallel. The insight of Justin was developed in more detail by Irenaeus of Lyons around 175 by showing in his *Adversus Haereses* how Jesus, the new Adam, retraced the steps of the old Adam in the undoing of the human race. This gave rise to similar references to Eve and Mary. Eve's disobedience was made the cause of death both for herself and the entire human race; but Mary, by yielding obedience, became the cause of salvation both for herself and the whole human race.

In Eastern Christian tradition, Origen of Alexandria about the year 250 delivered a series of sermons on the Gospel of St. Luke in which he declared Mary venerable by the divine childbearing and that through her all women were blessed. He also brings the Calvary scene of St. John's Gospel to bear as evidence that Jesus was Mary's only child. Following Origen, the role of Mary as model for Christian virgins would become increasingly important.

At the Latin-speaking end of the North African coast there lived Origen's older contemporary, Tertullian, who died in 221. Unlike Origen, Tertullian did not attribute any special sanctity to Mary. But he was a firm believer in the virgin conception and stressed the reality of Jesus' humanity.

All of these developments occurred prior to the Council of Nicaea in 325. They are significant in that they showed interest in and development of thinking about Mary for her own sake. This was to set the stage for the golden age of the Fathers, the fourth century between Nicaea in 325 and the Council of Ephesus in 431.

Preeminent in this period was St. Athanasius, who was to influence Western writers such as St. Ambrose in their thinking. Athanasius often used the Mary/Eve comparison/contrast to depict the condition of the human race. This period also witnessed the first undisputed usage of the term Theotokos to describe the position of Mary in history. The Cappadocian Fathers, Basil and the two Gregorys, developed this as well as the devotional aspects of Marian belief.

Interestingly, some of the lesser-known theologians of the period such as Epiphanius of Constantia provide us with much more insight into Marian thinking. Between 374 and 376 in the

Panarion, his compilation of heresies, he lists two dealing with Mary. The antidicomarianites (who were anti-Marian) and, at the other extreme, the Collyridians (who treat Mary as a goddess) supply a perfect balance for his treatise. The final pre-Ephesus Greek Father of great stature was St. John Chrysostom, priest of Antioch and bishop of Constantinople. He went into great detail in his homilies on the Annunciation and the Nativity, often in answer to the critics of Marian devotion.

The three great Western Fathers of the fourth century (Sts. Jerome, Ambrose, and Augustine) all had something to contribute. Jerome's major interest was in the area of Mary's virginity. Not surprisingly, as the foremost Scripture scholar of Christian antiquity, he engaged in a polemic with the Jews over the interpretation of Isaiah 7:14. Within the context of this polemic Jerome authored what has been called the first treatise on Mariology, *Adversus Helvidium.*

Ambrose's interests were somewhat broader than Jerome's. As the bishop of Milan he showed strong Marian devotion. In his work *De Institutione Virginis* he referred to Mary as the gate, of which it is written, "The Lord will pass through and it will be shut." The third great Latin Father, St. Augustine, would produce writings that would be vastly influential in setting forth both the teachings and problems that would confront Western theology. In his work titled *De Peccatorum Meritis et Remissione*, he stressed Mary's "Yes" to God's plan for her role in salvation history. Augustine believed that ultimately only God can do all things and that many of the things He actually does are beyond human comprehension. Overall, his Marian teachings are integrated into his total picture of salvation history.

Much has been said of the spread of Marian devotion after the Council of Ephesus in 431. The basis of such growth lies in the ancient traditions of the various Christian communities. The Assumption of the Blessed Virgin became a regular festival in many of these communities as early as the fifth century. By the sixth century, Emperor Maurice instituted the feast of Mary's Dormition on August 15. By the early seventh century, noteworthy sermons on the Assumption were being preached by Palestinian bishops such as Modestus of Jerusalem and Theoteknos of Livias. Marian piety and devotion came earlier and grew more rapidly in the East than it did in the West, but eventually it was to become a significant feature of faith in both areas of the early Church.

The writings of the Church Fathers are a valuable source of information concerning early Christian thinking about Mary. While those engaged in modern ecumenical discussions seem to focus primarily on either biblical sources or modern doctrinal statements, they would do well to consider the insights of these great pioneers of our faith as well.

Discussion Questions

1. Are you aware of any literature that makes a connection between Mary and Eve, particularly ideas that refer to Mary as the Second Eve?

2. Do you feel devotional practices surrounding Mary were a natural development of the Christian

community as opposed to regulations handed down by Church authorities?

3. Is it reasonable to believe that although devotional practices related to Mary were not explicitly spelled out in Scripture, they reflect the spirit of the Scriptures and are certainly not being done contrary to its teachings?

4

ଐ ✻ ଌ

Marian Tradition in the Early Church

A young boy returned home from a religion school class and announced to his mother that the teacher had talked about the Red Sea crossing. When his mother queried as to what the teacher said, the lad explained, "Well, Moses called up a division of men with howitzers to protect the shoreline, then radioed a fleet of torpedo-bearing subs for underwater support, and then used Hellcats and Spitfires for air support, and the whole troop movement to the other side was very successful." The shocked mother inquired, "Is that the way the teacher explained the Red Sea crossing to you?" "Not exactly," said the boy," but you'll never believe the story she did tell us!"

It was difficult for the mind of this young man to fathom the biblical writer's description of that event, so he sought to explain it in terms making sense to him. At the back of his mind was the assumption that he could fill in the details so as to make the story seem more realistic.

We often do the same with other events that make up Christian history. Certainly popular understandings about development of devotion to the Blessed Virgin Mary fall into this category. For those who haven't researched early documentation, there has always been an assumption that Marian devotion did not get under way in serious fashion until 431 with the Council of Ephesus, which declared her Theotokos, meaning God-bearer or Mother of God. In fact this very assumption, faulty as it is, has often been used by Protestants and others not sympathetic to such practices as a means of portraying Marian devotion as either an afterthought or an addition to the essential practice of Christian faith. Such skewed thinking had also served to perpetuate the false idea that liturgical practices are handed down by Church councils or other types of hierarchical decisions rather than seeing them in their true natural development as simply the fruit of long-standing devotional practices within the Christian communities.

A closer examination, however, of early Church writings clearly indicates that devotion to Mary has very deep roots in the early Church and far predate the Council of Ephesus. While Athanasius and, before him, Clement of Alexandria were dominant voices in support of Marian devotion in the second through the fourth centuries, there were even earlier evidences of a growing devotion to the Virgin. In the writings of Ignatius of Antioch (died c. 110) and Justin Martyr (died c. 165) we find statements that carry on the New Testament teachings about Mary. What Father Walter Brennan calls "memories" are actually creedal statements that imply professions of faith particularly at baptismal and eucharistic celebrations. In today's terminology we often call this "liturgy," but actually liturgy as we know and experience it nowadays was just beginning to take shape in the first-century Christian era. Baptism and the Eucharist were probably the earliest liturgical celebrations. They both laid heavy emphasis on the ancient Hebrew background to explain Christ to the early community of believers. And in the process of explaining Christ they incorporated His Mother. Jesus is both human and divine, but such doctrine was not automatically accepted by all Christians. There was a long rocky road to travel. For those who saw Christ as only divine, it was important for Church leaders to present the Incarnation and, of course, Mary as God's instrument in the Incarnation.

In the early second century, Justin Martyr looked back to Eve as a prefigurement of Mary. Both were virgins: Eve in the old creation and Mary in the new creation. If indeed liturgy is memory, there was a constant recollection of Mary in the early liturgy as Jesus' virgin Mother, as one who not only guaranteed the humanity of Jesus but also was part of God's eternal plan.

By the year 200, Irenaeus of Lyons developed further the parallel of Eve and Mary. Mary became an important part of the meditations and prayers of the people and their teachers. Irenaeus was a bishop and tried to unify Christians in various communities by his teachings. Evidently he felt his teaching about Mary would have been acceptable to Christians despite persecutions and the problems they faced. This emphasis on the unifying power of Mary for all Christian communities certainly seems to be one that is still worthy of consideration in our own day.

In the last years of the second century, Clement

of Alexandria, who taught in the famous catechetical school founded by his teacher Pantaneus, began to develop overlapping images between Mary and the Church. Eventually a meditative process began that resulted in joining these images. The Church on earth and the Church in glory were compared to Mary as the earthly Mother of Jesus and as a mother who was in glory due to holiness as the gift of salvation.

By the middle of the fourth century, Athanasius of Alexandria emerged. As secretary to the bishop of Alexandria he attended the ecumenical council at Nicaea in 325 and made many enemies by opposing the Arians, who denied that Jesus was both true God and true man. He will be remembered in Christian history for the brilliant way in which he united a theology of Christ to a theology of the Church. And Mary was very important to all of this. Devotion to Mary was not only a guarantee of the humanity of Jesus the Lord in our faith but also a memory of her special function in the working out of the plan of God for all time. For Athanasius, Mary is both the Theotokos and the model of the Christian life.

While Athanasius went to his eternal reward in the year 373, his work would influence the Council of Ephesus more than half a century later. By that time numerous Marian liturgical and devotional expressions were well-developed, and the people of the Christian communities had years of experience in using them. Thus Mary's titles of praise and explanation of her role in the Gospel developed rapidly. All this led to the official title of Theotokos being established at Ephesus in 431 and was actually the culmination of years of thinking, praying, praising, and, of course, experiencing.

It is important for us to gain such a glimpse into Marian devotion in the first three centuries following the apostolic age. This glimpse helps us to appreciate the steady pace of increasing recognition of the importance of Mary in the biblical record as well as in early tradition.

And finally, reviewing the documents of those early times helps us to answer the criticism of detractors of Marian devotion, both within and without the Church. We are led to understand that devotion to Mary, like so much else in Christian tradition, was not the result of some hastily made theological decision but the natural product growing out of the soil of years of human experience.

Discussion Questions

1. How has this chapter given you a new perspective on the development of Marian devotion?

2. How would you define "memories" in the context of Church history?

3. Are you aware of any liturgical practices in the Church today that are growing in popularity? Are they doing so because they meet a deep spiritual need?

5

✂ ✣ ✂

Theotokos:
The Rocky Road to Acceptance

It was a kind of media event, fifth-century style: crowds of people waiting outside a council hall in the ancient city of Ephesus. Then the verdict, reached behind closed doors, was announced to the public. In June of 431 the Council Fathers unanimously approved St. Cyril's doctrinal formulation of the Virgin Mary as the Theotokos, or the Mother of God.

One might think this was some kind of dreamy, irrelevant, or esoteric far-removed theological debate of interest only to scholars and Church dignitaries. Not so. When word came out to the crowd, eyewitness records to the event report that enthusiastic throngs surged through the streets of Ephesus, shouting over and over again, "Holy Mary, Mother of God!" Of course, their word for the second phrase was "Theotokos."

When the Church acknowledged this title of Mary, it was undoubtedly decisive for the growth in later centuries of Marian devotion and doctrine.

Like so much of Church doctrine, the Theotokos developed over several centuries as the Christian community recorded its experiences and began to articulate its beliefs. Among the earliest users of the term was Origen, who probably lived from 185 to 254. Between his time and the meeting at

Ephesus, those using the term to describe Mary reads like a *Who's Who?* of early Christianity and includes Archelaus of Mesopotamia, Eusebius of Palestine, and Alexander of Egypt in the third century. In the fourth century the list expanded to include Athanasius, Cyril of Palestine, Gregory of Nyssa and Gregory of Nazianzus (both in Cappadocia), plus Antiochus of Syria and Ammonius of Thrace, not to mention Emperor Julian. And another earlier emperor, Constantine, in his speech before the assembled bishops of Nicaea, used the explicit title "The Virgin Mother of God," which was also used by Ambrose of Milan, by Vincent and Cassian in France, and then by St. Leo.

The references to Mary were both frequent and eloquent. For example, St. Ignatius, who was martyred in 106, says, "Our God was carried in the womb of Mary." And Hippolytus observed, "The Word of God was carried in that Virgin frame." Others, such as Prochus, wrote, "God dwelt in the womb." Cassian observed that "Mary bore her Author," while Hilary wrote, "The one God only-begotten is introduced into the womb of a Virgin," and Ambrose exclaimed, "The Everlasting came into the Virgin."

But all this prolific rhetoric did not come about without some considerable dissension among the ranks of the Christian community. At the center of the early conflict was a fifth-century monk named Nestorius, who climbed the ranks of the Church to become patriarch of Constantinople.

Nestorius taught that there were two physical persons in Jesus Christ, not just one. One physical person was the Word of God and the second was the Son of David. The way this was possible, asserted Nestorius, was that the Word of God (divine) dwelt substantially in the Son of David (human). Thus, the Word of God never became a human, but only moved into and lived in a human.

Therefore Jesus Christ could not be called God, according to Nestorius, but only a God-carrier, that is, one in whom God dwelt. As far as Nestorius was concerned, you could call Mary the Christotokos (Mother of Christ), but you couldn't call her the Theotokos (Mother of God).

When word got to St. Cyril, bishop of Alexandria, that Patriarch Nestorius was preaching and teaching this doctrine, he proceeded to take Nestorius to task in sermons, letters, and writings that defended the Incarnation and the divine maternity.

Following an investigation of Nestorius's orthodoxy, a synod (presided over by Pope Celestine I) condemned the patriarch. The Pope sent Cyril to Nestorius to demand that he recant. This resulted in Emperor Theodosius I's convening the general Church Council of Ephesus, which set the stage for eventual approval of Bishop Cyril's thinking by the council.

Thus the road has been a rough one, but gradually the doctrine of the Theotokos has come to be accepted in the Church. As Cardinal John Henry Newman pointed out, "We cannot refuse the title to Mary without denying the Divine Incarnation — that is the great and fundamental truth of revelation, that God became man."

And now the understanding of the Blessed Virgin as the Theotokos begins to take on added importance in our present ecumenically-minded age. We refocus our understanding of the doctrine of God and man in one Person. All this sets the stage for new agreements based on sound doctrinal ground. It enables the Christian world to reiterate the fundamental teaching that Mary is the Theotokos, or Mother of God, and that Christ is our Immanuel, or God with us.

The road to such insights has, at times, been a bumpy one, but for the whole Church the destination has been worth the journey.

Discussion Questions

1. Do you feel religious doctrine to be more important to the laity in the early Church than it is in the modern Church?

2. How can the Church again restore the importance of doctrine to the life of its people?

6

ෂ ✕ ෨

What Luther Really Believed About Mary

After five centuries of Church history since the period of the Reformation, Catholics and Protestants alike assume the reformers downplayed the role of the Virgin Mary in God's plan of salvation. Actually the facts are otherwise. While it is true that many of the radical leaders who followed the original reformers sought to eliminate the Mother of our Lord from their theology, and in many cases were successful in all but doing so, this does not represent the position of the early leaders.

As pointed out in Chapter 2, Zwingli, for example, defended the use of Ave Maria as a means of rightful praise to the Blessed Virgin, and Calvin affirmed, "We cannot celebrate the blessings given us in Christ without commemorating at the same time, how high an honor God has granted to Mary when He chose to make her the Mother of His only Son." Yet today, despite these comments, followers of their traditions accord little position of honor to Mary in either theology or liturgical practice.

Perhaps in no other place is the discrepancy more evident than in the example of the viewpoints of Martin Luther contrasted with the practices and beliefs of modern Protestants. What did Luther really believe about Mary? For an answer to that question, we must search through his original writings.

Some interesting points emerge as a result of that investigation.

First, Luther referred to Mary as "the workshop of God" and decried Protestant antagonism toward her as an offshoot of Church conflict.

Luther believed in the help of the Virgin Mary for all worthwhile endeavors. In his letter to Prince John Frederick, duke of Saxony, in 1521 as a prologue to his commentary on the Magnificat of the first chapter of St. Luke's Gospel, he wrote, "May the tender Mother of God herself procure for me the spirit of wisdom profitably and thoroughly to expound this song of hers."

In the spirit of the Council of Ephesus of 431, he also continued to ascribe to her the title of Mother of God (Theotokos) and to refer to her as "Blessed."

Not only did Luther believe Mary helped Christians who call on her for assistance, he also supported prayers to her. Again, in his commentary on the Magnificat, he wrote, "O Blessed Virgin, Mother of God, what great comfort God has shown us in you by so graciously regarding your unworthiness and low estate."

For those who would follow in the faith, he desired a continued honor of Mary by stating, "The Virgin Mary means to say simply that her praise will be sung from one generation to another so that there will never be a time when she will not be praised."

While he was concerned about any beliefs or practices that might tend to make her equal with Christ in our redemption, in accord with Catholic theology throughout history, he referred to Mary as "Queen of Heaven" and called this a "true enough name."

Luther's belief in the position of Mary in salvation history is summed up in his conclusion to the commentary on the Magnificat where he states, "We pray God to give us a right understanding of this Magnificat, an understanding that consists not merely in brilliant words, but in glowing life in body and soul. May Christ grant us this through the intercession and for the sake of His dear Mother Mary."

Contrary to popular thought among both Catholics and Protestants, many of the reformers did not seek to devalue the place of the Virgin Mary in God's plan of salvation history. It was the people and events which followed that are primarily responsible for this unfortunate turn.

As the dialogue continues between Catholic and Protestant leaders, certainly both sides need to re-examine Luther's original writings. The honor he ascribed to the Blessed Virgin may indeed be a starting point for both fruitful discussion and greater understanding.

Discussion Questions

1. Why do you feel the later reformers departed from the attitudes of Martin Luther, John Calvin, and Huldrych Zwingli in their views about Mary?

2. Do your Protestant friends feel the Catholic Church places Mary on an equal footing with Christ?

3. What value might come from a restudy of the reformer's positions on Mary and a comparison with popular attitudes among Protestants today?

4. What kinds of meaningful joint observances could be shared between Catholics and Protestants in your community?

Some Present Understandings

Having set the stage for some basic comprehension of the backdrop of events leading to both beliefs about and practices surrounding Mary, we are now in a position to consider some present understandings. Among these are common human themes relating to motherhood, to reconciliation, to our songs of joy, and to our scientific explanations of the universe in which we live.

What better way to begin such a section than to consider the tenderness associated with the feminine image in contrast to the harshness that is so often a part of modern living?

7

⚿ ✳ ⚮

Mary: Model of Motherhood and Catholicity

In one of Victor Hugo's plays there is a scene in which a ship captain gives a starving mother and her two starving children a slice of bread. The mother promptly tears the slice in half and gives one piece to each child while taking nothing herself. A deckhand standing nearby turns to the captain and asks, "It is because she is not hungry, captain?" The captain replies, "No. It is because she is a mother."

In that dramatic episode, the great French playwright captured the depth of motherhood.

For millions of Christians, Mary is the universal mother of the Church. In her image of caring, sacrificing, and accepting responsibility, she elicits the same emotions among the faithful flock of Christ's Church as do our earthly mothers. The Church is the spiritual mother of Christians, and the Blessed Virgin is the mother of the Church. Her faithfulness to God's call and her acceptance of the responsibility He placed on her are a model for the Church in its need to be faithful to her Lord. According to Prior Roger Schutz of the Taizé Community in France, "The more the Church is in the image of Mary, the more it is like a mother."

For centuries before the coming of Christ there had existed, within the people of Israel, a community of humble believers in His coming. The Virgin Mary belonged to that community, whose members were mostly poor men and women who were eagerly looking forward to a fulfillment as they continued in faith to wait for the Messiah. By responding to the angel's announcement with a "yes," by her inward consent, Mary committed herself to a lifelong fidelity. "Behold, I am the handmaid of the Lord; let it be to me according to your word" (Luke 1:38). To accomplish His will, God asks us neither to destroy nor to exalt human desire but, in inner silence, to gather it up into an even greater desire: the passion for Christ and His Church.

Mother Teresa of Calcutta, through her life and words, reminds us, "The greatness of the Virgin Mary, like our own greatness, lies in humility. Even if people love us and appreciate our work, we must always remain humble, for our work is not ours, but God's work."

Martin Luther provided us with some insight into motherhood when he observed, "When Eve was brought unto Adam, he became filled with the Holy Spirit and gave her the most glorious of appellations. He called her Eva, that is to say, mother of all. He did not style her wife, but simply mother — mother of all living creatures." For the Church the Virgin Mary is the Second Eve. She is the mother of all who share in the new covenant made possible by the sacrifice of her Son on the cross.

Mary is the holy woman. In our day, that meaning has been covered over by centuries of male-centered symbols and meanings. For too long the Church has had a male-centered understanding of

Mary as "the successful woman" or "the powerful woman" or "the woman who meets our needs." Only rarely have we seen the image of Mary as the independent woman. She is the model of motherhood. As Thomas Carlyle wrote after watching his mother praying, "The highest whom I know on earth, I saw bowed down to a Higher in heaven." The English writer T. W. Higginson asked, "What are Raphael's Madonnas, but the shadow of a mother's love fixed in permanent outline forever?"

Mary is present among us as our model and mother. She is there with Christ, but it is up to us whether she stays. St. Augustine once said as he searched for God in his memory, "You were with me, but I was not with You." It is up to us to be with Mary so that she stays with us.

If Mary is the model of motherhood, she is also the model of catholicity (that is, universality). Even as earthly mothers are so often the symbol of that which holds human families together, so she is the great symbol of the whole Christian family. Again, Prior Roger Schutz of Taizé counsels us with the thought, "In Mary we can glimpse two realities essential for the Church and closely linked to one another — motherhood and catholicity. If one of these realities disappears, the other also begins to fade away."

In our time, we are still faced with the tragic divisions among the world's Christians. Yet, standing on the brink of a bright new ecumenical age, Mary as the model of catholicity, or universality, becomes even more important. In the course of many centuries from the beginning of the Church, from the time of Mary and the Apostles, the motherhood of the Church was one. This fundamental motherhood cannot vanish, even though divisions occur. Mary, through her motherhood, maintains the catholicity of Christ's flock. As the entire Christian community turns to her, the possibility of a new birth, a reconciliation, increases. So Mary, the mother of the Church, is also a source of reconciliation among her scattered and divided children.

Since the first Pentecost the figure of Mary has been a transparent image of the Church. With the Apostles she was able to understand that, in Christ, ". . . the grace of God has appeared for the salvation of all men" (Titus 2:11). In her there is a catholicity of heart.

As Father Walter Brennan has written, "The insistent realization of our time is globalization. Every human being is, in several ways, dependent upon other human brings. The fact of this globalization or world interdependence is also related to faith. Mary shows how this world interdependence relates to our faith."

Thus Vatican Council II was on target when it exhorted, "Joined to Christ the Head and in common with all His saints, the faithful must in the first place, reverence the memory of the glorious ever-Virgin Mary, Mother of God and of our Lord, Jesus Christ."

Somewhere there is a story about a schoolboy who misspelled a greeting card with the words "Mary Christmas." When told to correct this he proceeded to write, "Marry Christmas." When asked again to correct the spelling, he finally wrote it as "Merry

Christmas." For Christians, should not all three spellings be regarded as correct? It is a "Mary Christmas" because the Virgin gave birth to the world's Savior. It is also a "Marry Christmas" because our Lord has claimed the Church as His holy bride. Now, because of the first two spellings, we can all rejoice in the Nativity of Jesus, our Lord, and truly celebrate a "Merry Christmas."

Thus Mary continues to be for the entire Christian community the model of both motherhood and catholicity and, through these images, the great reconciler of that community.

Discussion Questions

1. How may the life of Mary be portrayed as a model for motherhood in our own day?

2. What might be some common meeting ground for Protestants and Catholics in beliefs about Mary?

3. What can we learn from ecumenical communities like the Taizé in France about ways of understanding Mary both in life and in worship?

4. How can a deeper understanding of Mary give us a new perspective on the meaning of vocation?

5. How does Mary contribute to a better understanding of the dignity of women?

8

ঙ �֎ ৬

Mary in Protestant Hymnology

The faith of the Church is often expressed at least as much in its liturgy and hymns as in its doctrinal statements. For the parishioner in the pew, it is not obscure dogmatic statements issued by theologians at far-removed councils and conferences but rather the regular acts of praise and worship that determine his or her religious faith. The ancient Latin axiom "lex orandi, lex credendi" continues to be a true expression, for as we worship, so do we believe.

The story of Protestant hymnology tells a story about Protestant belief concerning the Virgin Mary that is seldom expressed in theological statements. From the earliest liturgy one of the best-loved hymns of the Christian community has been "Mary's Song" or, more properly, "The Magnificat" of Luke 1:46-55. Like so many Mariological practices in the Church, this great hymn is sung by all Christians, not for glorification of the Virgin Mary, but as a means of directing us to Christ.

Today "The Magnificat" exists in over twenty-three hundred English-language versions. These include the Gospel canticle in Evening Prayer present in many Protestant liturgies that reads, "My soul proclaims the greatness of the Lord." It is also found in hymns with stanzas such as: "My soul now magnifies the Lord / My spirit leaps for joy in Him / He keeps me in His kind regard / And I am blest for time to come."

Whether Protestants realize it or not, hymns to the Blessed Mother of our Lord are also present in their hymnology. They are both Mariological and Christological. In the Christmas hymn "Angels We Have Heard On High," there is a stanza from that traditional French carol that reads: "See Him in a manger laid / Whom the angels praise above / Mary, Joseph, lend your aid / While we raise our hearts in love."

Another popular Protestant hymn used on All Saints' Day (November 1) is entitled "Ye Watchers and Ye Holy Ones" and contains the following words: "O Higher than the cherubim / More glorious than the seraphim / Lend their praises, Alleluia / The bearer of the Eternal Word / Most gracious magnify the Lord — Alleluia."

Here we appeal to Mary as the mediatrix, a voice that speaks for us in heaven. She is invoked as "most gracious."

A very meaningful Lenten hymn present in many Protestant hymnals is the beautiful "At the Cross Her Station Keeping." The entire hymn, generally five stanzas, focuses on Mary's faith as a role model for all Christians. One verse is particularly powerful: "Who on Christ's dear mother gazing / Pierced at anguish so amazing / Born of woman, would not weep? / Who, on Christ's dear mother thinking / Such a cup of sorrow drinking / Would not share her sorrows deep?"

The liturgical calendar also tells a tale. Hymnology develops from the liturgical calendar. Many

Protestants celebrate August 15 as the feast of Mary, Mother of our Lord, which is celebrated in the Roman Catholic Church as the feast of the Assumption. This feast was incidentally recommended by Martin Luther as a continuing evidence of the evangelical catholic faith. In addition, the feasts of the Annunciation (March 25) and the Visitation (May 31) are also observed in some Protestant circles. Since both of these events took place prior to the first Christmas, the Roman Catholic Church has a good argument in claiming them as Marian feasts as well as claiming the whole of Advent season as a Marian season.

Invocation of the Virgin Mary and other saints is, interestingly enough, not forbidden in some Protestant groups. For example, the Augsburg Confession of the Lutheran Church states explicitly that such practices are neither forbidden nor required.

Through our hymns and in our liturgical practices there runs a great hope for ecumenical understanding. Mary is the archetype of the Church. In the opening chapters of the Lucan Gospel, she is presented as the obedient handmaiden of God. St. Luke portrays her as being what the Church should be: submissive to the divine will and receptive to the divine call.

Let us rejoice with Mary that we the Church have been chosen to be this obedient servant. Let us say as the Mother of our Lord said to the archangel Gabriel in Luke 1:38: "Behold, I am the handmaid of the Lord; let it be to me according to your word."

Through the hymns of the Church, Protestants

already affirm what most Catholics believe concerning Mary. The time has come to stop quibbling over our differences and begin rejoicing in what we share.

Discussion Questions

1. Are you aware of any Church music or special anthems on the Virgin Mary that might be acceptable to Protestants?

2. Do your Protestant friends generally feel the "Ave Maria" to be an objectionable hymn?

3. What popular hymns can you think of that may have a unifying effect among both Catholics and Protestants?

4. Check through some Protestant hymnals. You will be surprised to find so many hymns that mention Mary.

9

ॐ ✼ ♋

Mary:
Key to Understanding Science

Most Americans have either heard of or read about the famous "Scopes Trial," which took place in Dayton, Tennessee, in 1925. John Scopes, a public schoolteacher in that town, was arrested for teaching evolution in the classroom. His efforts, though represented by the famous labor attorney Clarence Darrow, were defeated when the court ruled in favor of the school board, represented by the Protestant fundamentalist and political leader William Jennings Bryan.

The impact of the decision that day was to be felt far beyond the borders of that small town and far beyond the year of 1925. The Scopes case — sometimes called the "monkey trial" — continues to be debated, and the decision laid down that day has settled little; indeed it has proved to be a jumping-off point toward further debate. (At the time of the trial, Tennessee law allowed the teaching of creationism only. The law was abolished in 1967.)

Over the ensuing seven decades since the trial, science textbooks have gradually incorporated evolution in their contents as at least one theory to explain the descent of the human race while making no particular effort to either dissuade or convince students of a religious faith.

Interestingly, this controversy of science versus

religion has involved primarily Protestant fundamentalist groups who, holding on to a rigid biblicism, feel threatened by suggestions of the scientific community that there may be ways of explaining the biological processes whereby human beings have arrived at the point we now are. The battles of this century between science and Protestant fundamentalists have certainly involved the problem of how to talk about God being above and before the world and yet in the world amidst the processes of nature.

It is at this point that the position of the Blessed Virgin Mary becomes a prime importance. For Catholics and all others who will consider it, a mature view of Mary in God's plan of creation provides us with a key to understanding science, while at the same time relieving us of the problem of involvement in the age-old controversies between science and religion.

Even Protestant historian Jaroslav Pelikan admits this in his book *The Riddle of Roman Catholicism* when he observes that the insight of the Catholic Church into Mariology has enabled it "to incorporate a full-blown view of the world of nature into its system without sacrificing the sovereign otherness of God." Such an honest recognition of the important role of Mary as the Mother of God helps us to understand how a loving God used the processes of the natural world to become one with His creation. This is the glorious mystery of the Incarnation, which occurs through the vehicle of the flesh of the Blessed Virgin. Thus, in the Holy Eucharist we come not to celebrate a vague spirit but to partake of the holy Body and Blood of Jesus, her Son.

So God did not send us an idea, however lofty that idea may be. He sent His Only-Begotten Son born of Mary's flesh. Understanding and believing this makes it easier to appreciate how God continually works in and through the processes of nature. Hence there can be no real conflict between science and religion. The nineteenth-century clergyman Edward Chain captured this thought when he said, "Through all God's works, there runs a beautiful harmony. The remotest truth in His universe is linked to that which lies nearest the throne."

At the risk of oversimplification, we may venture to say that religion answers the *who* of life while science struggles with the *how*. Both have the same Divine Author.

The conflicts of the past seventy years since the Scopes Trial continue to pop up in our newspapers as local skirmishes emerge between groups often polarized as combatants in a gang fight. Often there are those of science who equate religion with superstition and those of religion who equate science with unbelief. In the light of the Incarnation, both miss the point.

We pray for the day when people of broad minds and good will in both science and religion will take center stage to set the record straight. The famous American jurist Oliver Wendell Holmes foresaw such a happening when he commented, "As knowledge advances, science ceases to scoff at religion and religion ceases to frown on science. The hour of mockery by the one and reproof by the other is passing away. Henceforth they will dwell together in unity and good will. They will mutually illustrate the wisdom, power, and grace of God. Science will adorn and enrich religion and religion will ennoble and sanctify science."

Of course that day of which the judge spoke has yet to arrive, as volatile confrontations continue to erupt.

Some historians suggest that such conflicts have occurred as the result of the lack of a mature Mariology, particularly among the Protestant groups. So Protestantism has been caught up in the dilemma of either stressing the involvement of God in nature too directly, which dilutes the concept of God to mere process, or emphasizing the lordship and otherness of God to the point of abstracting Him from the natural process. Father Yves M. J. Congar believes this is the natural result of a disregard for "the role of humanity in salvation." In his text *A Study in Irenic Theology*, he states his belief that Protestant emphasis on the divine nature of Christ only, while largely ignoring the human nature, has led to such conflict and the emergence of a provincial outlook that erects artificial categories between the two areas. For those of us who yearn to see bridges built, a recognition of the dual natures of our Lord and a recognition of divine operations in the context of the natural world are both absolutely essential.

For Christians, God is not an idea but a Person who comes to us in the flesh through His Divine Son. The Blessed Virgin is the agent of the Incarnation. Therefore God can be above the processes of nature as well as the One who acts within them.

The Incarnation through Mary both enriches religion and ennobles science.

The seventeenth-century cleric Philip Henry asserted, "The person who thinks there can be any real conflict between science and religion must be either very young in science or very ignorant in religion."

As Pope Pius XI so rightfully observed, "Those who speak of the incompatibility of science and religion either make science say that which is never said or make religion say that which it never taught."

Let us hope that all Christians will recognize the importance of the Virgin Mary and the fact that God chose the form of human flesh to reveal His love. Then the artificial gap between science and religion will disappear and together we shall sing our Te Deums to Him who is the Author of both.

Discussion Questions

1. What do you know about the Scopes Trial and the issues that were debated there?

2. Have you or other members of your family read articles in biology books that deal with this subject?

3. Has the creationism-evolutionism debate been oversimplified by both newspaper and religious groups? Are there other options to an either/or approach?

4. Can Christians regard evolution as a possible explanation for life on earth as we know it now while still maintaining a firm belief in God?

10

✄ ✄ ✄

Our Universal Mother: Mary Has Appeal to Many Cultures

A Muslim student visiting Rome wants especially to see the Church of Santa Maria Maggiore. Surprised? The poetry of a Syrian mystic is replete with Marian devotion. Surprised? Martin Luther recommended prayer to Mary. Surprised? An American Pentecostalist minister begins to visit shrines of Marian apparitions. Surprised? Muslims refer to Mary as il-Sittneh, or Our Lady. Surprised? A chapter in the Koran is named after her. Surprised? Mary's deep kindness as a mother is portrayed in Chinese art. Surprised? And now a Presbyterian minister has written a book recommending the praying of the Rosary. Still surprised?

While the above events may come under the general classification of surprises, or perhaps even shock to some, they hold one thing in common — all are factual. Devotion to, or even recognition of, the importance of Mary has often been thought of as being the exclusive province of the Catholic Church in most people's minds. But a closer investigation of both past history and current events points out that Mary has a universal appeal that transcends our cultural, geographic, and even religious boundaries.

To understand the reason for this, we need to examine the responses of people from different ages of time and from different traditions that make up our world culture.

We may begin with the example of the Muslim tourist in Rome desiring to visit the most famous of that ancient city's Marian shrines. He explained to his host, a Catholic journalist, how his religion admired the humiliation and the misunderstanding Mary had to face when she accepted the mission of bringing Jesus into the world. Then he added, "Because of this she understands everything we have to face in life."

With this explanation he touched on one factor in the universal appeal of the Blessed Mother of our Lord — the element of tenderness. What adult is there among us who can't remember those moments of his or her childhood when what was needed most was the tenderness of a caring mother who displayed understanding amidst a moment of hurt or fright? I remember once reading a story about a small boy who got separated from his mother in a train station. He began to cry and scream for her. Passersby attempted to comfort him by offering him candy and toys while they were searching for his mother. But all such offerings failed to assuage his fears. Material pleasures just wouldn't do it; only the sight of a loving mother would solve the problem.

While at least one deep emotional need in most of our lives has been that of having a loving mother, so our religious needs find fulfillment in the world's mother — the Blessed Virgin Mary, bearer of the Christ Child.

Seeking further reasons for the universal appeal of Mary takes us from the scene of a Muslim tourist to the changed beliefs of a fundamentalist Protestant minister. Raised amidst the prejudices and suspicions that often accompany training in this tradition, he gradually began to overcome such long-held prejudices while an observer at the Second Vatican Council. In fact he became so taken up by his realization of the importance of devotion to Mary that he would later make pilgrimages to several sites of Marian apparitions and share in the joy of the many pilgrims who come to them.

But rising above entrenched and often unfounded suspicions in Protestant traditions is not new with this twentieth-century Pentecostalist clergyman. Back in the sixteenth century, Martin Luther, despite his differences with the Church of his day, recommended devotion to Mary and even published some extensive studies on the Magnificat.

Our journey in search of answers to the universal appeal of Mary now takes a turn from the scene of twentieth-century Western Protestantism to the early centuries of Russian Christianity. The Orthodox tradition has produced some of the most beautiful icons and paintings ever that depict the Mother of our Lord. When the fifth-century Council of Ephesus proclaimed Mary as the Theotokos (Mother of God), poets and artists of the Eastern Orthodox world would literally seek to outdo one another in her praise. The liturgy of the Eastern Church is woven together with cycles of ancient Marian hymns incomparable for their blend of poetic, scriptural, and theological insight. And such world-famous icons as the tenth-century Virgin of Vladimir in the

Treyakov Gallery of Moscow and the thirteenth-century Panagia Virgin are standard entries in textbooks depicting great world art.

So the evidence is indeed surprising, or perhaps shocking, to some that the Virgin Mary should enjoy such widespread acceptance among such culturally divergent groups. Yet it shouldn't be a surprise. No eyebrows ought to be raised when we stop and reflect on how she embodies so much of our universal human longings: the desire for tenderness and understanding as well as the caring for all her children — all qualities we associate with motherhood.

Perhaps the Muslim tourist expressed it best when he replied to his Catholic journalist friend, "So you think that the Virgin Mary belongs only to you Catholics. Don't you know she is the mother of the whole world?"

When we reflect on the image of a Jewish maiden held in reverence by the Islamic faith; the subject of much scholarly writing by a German reformer; depicted in the art of the Chinese; painted in icons and sung in chant by the Russian Orthodox; and discovered meaningful by American Pentecostals and Presbyterians, we begin to realize devotion to Mary knows no boundaries. We begin to recognize that she is indeed the mother of the world.

Discussion Questions

1. Have you ever talked to a person who belonged to a non-Christian religion about his or her views on Mary?

2. Do you detect a universal quest for some el-

ements of tenderness in religions that often appear, at least on the surface, to be harsh and judgmental?

3. What do you know about the place of Mary in Eastern Orthodox Christianity? Is it much different from Catholic beliefs?

Connecting Past and Present

The connecting link between past and present is kept alive by ancient liturgical practices. In this section we will review some of the major Marian feasts and their relevance to Christian dialogue. Hopefully the readers will gain new insights both into the rationale for these practices and also into the ways they can serve as bridges to understanding.

We begin with an overall look at Marian festivals in the life of the Church and then proceed to handle five of them in greater detail, finally closing out this part of the book with a look at the Rosary.

11

⊿ ✂ ⍅

The Marian Feasts:
Celebrations for All Christians

The mention of Marian feasts in the Church's liturgy immediately causes the Protestant mind to assume they are only of interest to Catholic clergy and laity. What is overlooked in this hasty assumption are some very important facts that need to be reexamined by all Christian churches. Contrary to what many non-Catholics assume without due investigation, Marian feasts (1) have a biblical basis, (2) are ancient in origin, (3) point us to Christ, and (4) glorify the Holy Trinity.

For these reasons the entire Christian world needs to reconsider the need for including feasts of the Virgin Mary in its worship schedule. A closer look at seven Marian feasts shows why this is so.

❦ The Immaculate Conception (December 8). This is a celebration that dates back to the eighth century and relates to St. Anne's conception of Mary. St. Anselm, who became bishop of Canterbury in 1093, summed up the importance of this feast in his prayer, "Lady full and overflowing with grace; all creation receives new life from your abundance." For St. Anselm and other early Christian writers, without the Son of God nothing could possibly exist; and without Mary's Son, nothing could be redeemed. The center of thought is therefore on creation in the sense that everything as a result of the fruit of Mary's womb is restored to its original beauty. So this feast, in the final analysis, contains a message of redemption.

❦ The Nativity of the Blessed Virgin (September 8). This feast was set by the early Church at nine months after the Immaculate Conception. St. Andrew of Crete has enriched the Church with some beautiful homilies on this feast. For him this event is a prelude to the final act, the union of the Word with flesh. The feast celebrates the fact that the Virgin is "born, tended, and formed" in order to be prepared for her eminent role as God's Mother. Again, here is a feast that points to the Incarnation of God in Christ.

❦ The Presentation of Mary (November 21). This celebration draws upon the apocryphal story of Mary's presentation in the Temple as a child. The fourth-century Church Father St. Augustine comments, "She who believed by faith, conceived by faith." He then expands on this by saying, "And so it was for her a greater thing to have been Christ's disciple than to have been His Mother. Her happiness was that she bore in her womb Him whom she would obey as her master." And so, we have yet another example of an ancient Marian feast that points to Christ.

❦ The Annunciation (March 25). A feast that occurs nine months before Christmas, it focuses on the angel's announcement to Mary of the future birth of Christ through her and the Holy Spirit. Pope St. Leo the Great, writing in the middle of the fifth century, spoke of "the mystery of man's reconciliation with God." This feast reminds us that He who participated in the nature of God and had created man became, in the nature of a servant, man himself. So the feast of the Annunciation not only helps us to better understand the nature of the Holy Trinity, it also directs our thoughts to the Christmas Incarnation.

❦ The Visitation (May 31). Dating from the Middle Ages, this celebration reenacts the scriptural account of Mary's visit to her kinswoman Elizabeth, who is about to give birth to St. John the Baptist. St. Bede the Venerable, writing in the seventh century, reminds us that in this feast "Mary proclaims the greatness of the Lord working in her." This is especially important, for there we see the Mother of God as a creature who proclaims God's greatness and knows that He who is the source of eternal salvation would be brought into this world by her. Thus, this feast contains the mark of salvation in Christ.

❦ The Presentation of the Lord (February 2). This feast marks the end of the Christmas season and is also known as Candlemas Day because of the tradition of blessing candles on this day. It observes the Presentation of the Lord in the Temple. St. Sophronius, a monk of the seventh century, takes up the theme by exhorting, "Let us receive the light whose brilliance is eternal." This was also known as the feast of the Purification of the Blessed Virgin, since the legal cleansing ritual occurred at the same time. Again, by means of a Marian feast, the Son of God is exalted.

❦ The Assumption. This is the last of the Marian feasts and dates from the fourth century. It is a celebration of the death and taking into heaven of our Lady. St. Germanus of Constantinople, an eighth-century Church Father, wrote, "Her virginal body is entirely holy, entirely chaste, entirely the house of God." Interestingly, Martin Luther, during the reformation period of the sixteenth century, included the feast of the Assumption on a list of liturgical celebrations that should "be observed among Evangelical Catholics as a sign of continuity and order."

So it is evident from the history of the Church's celebration of the above seven Marian feasts that they have a biblical basis, are ancient in origin, point us to Christ, and glorify the Holy Trinity. Therefore they belong to — and ought to be celebrated by — all those who claim Christ as Savior and Lord. God's ways of revealing Himself to us emerge from these great traditions. Mary's moments are special moments in which God speaks to His covenant people.

These are not therefore feasts whose design is some type of deification of Mary, although they certainly accord her the honor she deserves. An honest look at their history and development shows us that in honoring the Blessed Virgin, we give praise to her Son, our Savior.

As one Trappist abbot used to say to his monks, "All for Jesus through Mary with a smile."

Discussion Questions

1. Does your parish celebrate as many Marian feasts now as it has in the past? Has there been a lesser or greater emphasis on these feasts?

2. Do you know of Protestant congregations in your area that are observing any of the Marian feasts? Episcopal and Lutheran congregations would be the most likely as well as, of course, Eastern Orthodox parishes.

3. Why are Marian feasts, when properly understood, really celebrations that point to Christ?

4. Make a list of some of the Marian feasts that you think would not be objectionable to most Protestant congregations.

12

ॐ ✹ ℞

The Thrill of a New Beginning: The Annunciation

Early one morning in the year 1811 the city of Paris was awakened by the roar of cannons and gun salutes. It was a way of announcing to all of France that Napoleon had a son. Most births are not accompanied by such dramatic announcements. Most of the greatest human beings who ever lived came into the world under much more quiet conditions; many were born in ordinary circumstances, some even in poverty.

Contrast the above fanfare with the world's greatest announcement of a birth-to-be — the Annunciation by the archangel Gabriel to the Blessed Virgin that she had been chosen by God to bear His Son. Of all the festivals that center on the position of Mary in Christian tradition, with the exception of Christmas, none is so universally accepted by the Christian community as that of the Annunciation. Set by the Church as March 25, it occurs nine months before Christmas and focuses on the angel's announcement of the future birth of the Christ Child. While Catholic and Eastern Orthodox traditions have always emphasized this feast through liturgical celebration, most Protestant groups tend to ignore any special celebrations of it.

Although some Anglicans and Lutherans recognize the importance of the feast, it is beginning to gain wider acceptance among Christians in general. And well it should. Perhaps no other Marian feast provides us with so much insight into the personality of the Blessed Mother of our Lord and gives us more reason to honor her.

There are at least three emotions that Mary displayed when confronted with the glorious announcement. She was afraid, she was curious, and she was willing. A closer look at each of these emotions and the manner in which she handled them provides all Christians with ample reasons for honoring her.

1. Mary was afraid. The announcement had to have caught her off guard. She must have been afraid of becoming a mother — and an unwed one at that. She knew she would have to face the gossip of the community in shame and disgrace. Moreover, she must have been afraid of what her fiancé, Joseph, would do, as well as of the nasty stories that were sure to circulate in the community about her.

Mary had many reasons to fear the announcement. But it turned out to be fear in terms of awe, reverence, and respect in the presence of the messenger from God. The solution to this fear was what the angel said to her, "Do not be afraid, Mary. You have found favor with God."

If God is only a God of justice and wrath, you and I need to fear Him. But, in truth, He comes to us personally and wants to be born in us, because He loves us. He accepts us and makes us His children, coming not to harm or condemn but to bless and to save.

Mary dealt with her fear when she came to understand this and, as such, she is the Christian's model for dealing with fear.

2. Mary was curious. Once the announcement had been made that she was to have a baby, she responded with: "How can this be, since I have no husband?" That was the cue for Gabriel to explain to Mary that the father of the child would be the Holy Spirit. No man can either take credit or be blamed for her pregnancy.

I remember hearing a humorous line, although perhaps not intentional, in a church Christmas pageant. Mary and Joseph were asking for a room in the inn. The innkeeper asked, "Can't you see the 'No Vacancy' sign?" Joseph replied, "Yes, but can't you see that my wife is expecting a baby any minute?" The innkeeper retorted, "Well that's not my fault!" Joseph responded, "Well, it's not mine either."

The Annunciation upholds the Church's teaching of the virgin birth. Jesus' birth was totally the work of God. "How can this be?" is a familiar question of humans. At age ninety, Sarah was told by God she would give birth. She laughed and asked that question. Nicodemus, who came to Jesus by night, was told he must be born again. He responded with the same curious question.

Now Mary is to have a child without a husband. But the angel reminds her, and she in turn reminds us, that with God all things are possible. So Mary's curiosity, which surrenders to faith, then becomes a model for every Christian who would ask how the Christ Child can be born anew in him or her. If

Christ is born in us, we have the spirit of Christ in us: a spirit of love, goodness, and mercy. The curiosity and subsequent faith of the Blessed Mother of our Lord remains a model for the entire Christian world.

3. Mary was willing. Finally, Mary's reaction to the angel's announcement that she would give birth to the Son of God was one of acceptance. "Behold I am the handmaid of the Lord; let it be to me according to your word" (Luke 1:38). She accepted the miracle of the virgin birth gladly, although she felt unworthy of the high calling.

A few years ago when baseball star Dave Winfield was traded from the San Diego Padres to the New York Yankees, he became the highest paid player in baseball history. One newspaper account showed him pictured with his proud mother, who had raised him and his brother by herself. Now suppose she had dreamed her son would make more money than Babe Ruth. She would have possibly shrugged it off as an "impossible dream." Yet, like Mary, she would have found the incredible news too good to be true but at the same time too good to be rejected.

If God was to send His Son to earth, He had to have the acceptance and cooperation of Mary. She cheerfully and obediently submitted to His will. Her body became the instrument by which He would enter the world as a human being.

So too, if Christ is to be born in us, we need to offer our bodies as instruments in carrying out His will. This calls for submission and dedication. Mary shows us what God can do with our lives when we are willing to submit to His design.

In Mary's human emotions of fear, curiosity, and acceptance, we learn how to deal with our own. For this reason, the feast of the Annunciation needs to be reemphasized in various Catholic traditions and reborn in Protestant ones.

Discussion Questions

1. Does your parish place any emphasis on the celebration of the feast of the Annunciation?

2. Do you know of any Episcopal or Lutheran parishes in your area that also observe this feast?

3. What qualities of human personality can we learn from Mary's response to the Annunciation?

4. Would a joint celebration between your parish and a Protestant congregation be meaningful? If so, what common elements might be emphasized?

13

⚘ ✶ ⚘

Sharing the Joy: The Visitation

Nothing seems to produce more joy in a family than the realization that a baby is on the way. The soon-to-be parents want to share the news with anyone who will listen. At times we may also have been in the company of two women, both of whom were preparing for childbirth, listening to them compare notes on their feelings, their anxieties, their expectations, and their hopes.

Such a scene was enacted in the record of St. Luke's Gospel in which he describes the visit of the Virgin Mary to St. Elizabeth, who was to become the mother of St. John the Baptist (see Luke 1:39-55). The event is celebrated in the Church as simply "The Visitation," and the feast date has been designated as May 31.

The event described in the Gospel follows on the heels of two great announcements. First, there was the news brought to Zechariah that his wife, Elizabeth, was to give birth to a son who was to fulfill a special assignment in God's plan. During Elizabeth's pregnancy the archangel Gabriel would then appear to Mary announcing that she would give birth to Jesus, the Savior.

The feast of the Visitation dates from the Middle Ages and reenacts the scriptural account of the visit of Mary to her kinswoman Elizabeth to share the joy of two annunciations. This feast is recognized in many parts of the universal Christian community, which includes Anglicans, Lutherans, and Eastern Orthodox as well as Catholics, although, unfortunately, it does not receive much liturgical attention in the first two groups. The Visitation is both a Marian feast and a feast of salvation history and therefore important for all Christians. St. Bede the Venerable, writing in the seventh and eighth centuries, sums up for us the theme of this feast: "Mary proclaims the greatness of the Lord working in her."

There are interesting parallels between this visit and two other visits recorded in the Old Testament. First, the Gospel writer describes the unborn John as leaping in his mother's womb when Mary pays her visit. We recall the births of Esau and Jacob from Rebekah in the twenty-fifth chapter of Genesis. Jacob was, of course, to become the father of the Israelites from whose line would come the Christ Child. The scriptural principle here indicates that one's later role in salvation history can be foreshadowed by prenatal behavior. The second great parallel with earlier biblical history is centered on Elizabeth's surprise that Mary, carrying the future Messiah, should visit her. We recall the surprise expressed by Araunah in 2 Samuel 24 at the fact that David would visit his home. Now, here in St. Luke's Gospel, the Mother of the Davidic King pays a visit and shares a common joy.

We celebrate the feast of the Visitation because it brings together two annunciations. St. Luke carefully portrays the Annunciation of Jesus as having a much greater role in our salvation than that of

John. By recording that the unborn John leaps in Elizabeth's womb, St. Luke indicates how John acknowledges the superiority of Jesus, his Lord.

It is important for this feast to be recognized and celebrated in the Church. Like other great liturgical events, it is designed to nourish us in our faith. Using a very human scene, so common to our everyday experience, God assures us again, through the Church's celebration, that He has not forgotten His people of this or any other age.

The Visitation is the sharing of a common joy — the joy expressed between two of God's chosen vessels and the joy that is a loving Father's gift to all His children. The Visitation is a Marian feast in the Church's calendar. Like all Marian feasts, it is also a celebration of the hope we all have in God's acts of salvation through our Blessed Lord.

Discussion Questions

1. How much emphasis is there on the feast of the Visitation in your parish?

2. Are you aware of any local Protestant (particularly Episcopal or Lutheran) congregations that also recognize this feast?

3. Would a joint celebration with them be feasible?

4. What distinctly human elements of family life can be emphasized from a celebration of this feast?

14

☙ ✼ ❧

Mothers Have Birthdays Too: The Nativity of Mary

Unlike the feasts of the Assumption and the Immaculate Conception, the feast of the Nativity of the Blessed Virgin Mary has not ignited the fires of controversy among non-Catholics. However, while this feast has not become a focus of contention, it is a celebration that is, for the most part, ignored by non-Catholics. Some Anglicans and Lutherans will recognize the feast if it happens to fall on a Sunday and is therefore read from the pericopes for the day, but they generally give little emphasis to it.

Since Christ's birthday is celebrated, so Mary too ought to be honored on her birthday, which is placed nine months after the Immaculate Conception. As mentioned in an earlier chapter, St. Andrew of Crete in the eighth century enriched the Church with some beautiful homilies devoted to the Blessed Mother. His theme on this feast is "the old has passed away — all things are made new." For St. Andrew this event is a prelude to the "final act" of the union of the Word with flesh. It sets the stage for the Incarnation of our Lord. Mary is prepared for her eminent role as God's Mother. The creature is newly prepared to be a divine dwelling place for the Creator.

All Christians gather to celebrate Christmas as

the birthday of our Lord, but few recognize the birthday of the Blessed Virgin Mary, His Mother. Let us remember that mothers have birthdays too.

There is an interesting account of mission work in the slums of a large city in which Protestant missionaries began teaching religion to the children by telling them God was their heavenly Father. While there was nothing wrong with this from a theological perspective, it completely backfired from an emotional one. The word "father" conjured up feelings of fear and disgust. So many had fathers whom they could remember as coming home in a drunken state and being abusive to them and their mothers. A religion related to a father image didn't seem to be very inviting. At the same time, the Catholic missionaries were much more successful in teaching these inner-city youngsters by relating religion to Mary our mother. Since "mother" symbolized that one person on whom they could count, it was much easier for them to accept religious teaching surrounding her.

This episode serves to point out what has often been a missing ingredient in non-Catholic traditions. In their totally masculine orientation, they have sometimes developed a harshness while people are crying out for a little tenderness in their religious faith. And what could portray this tenderness any better than the affection shown by the Blessed Mother of our Lord for her Son and, with it, the affection she conveys to all of us who are His followers?

Even modern psychology has recognized this flaw in our thinking. For years we were told not to allow boys to play with dolls, fearing it would make them effeminate. Now we have come to recognize that boys, no matter how rugged they are, need some balance. Hugging dolls and Teddy Bears teaches them the qualities of affection they need in order to develop into well-balanced adults. I am reminded of the recent emergence of an all-pro National Football League lineman and a Hall of Fame baseball star, both of whom are involved in the flower industry. They have taught us that one can be a man among men, as they certainly are, and yet show appreciation for the tender side of life.

September 8 has been set by the Church as the day on which we commemorate the birthday of the Blessed Virgin Mary. It is a commemoration that should belong to the entire Church. Our Lady belongs to all of us. In honoring her Nativity, we not only emphasize an element of warmth and tenderness in religion, we also point out how God sometimes chooses unexpected ways to show His glory. What could be more unexpected than His choosing of the Mother of His Son, not from the ranks of royalty, but from the community of a captive and often impoverished people? So Mary could truthfully say, ". . . he has regarded the low estate of his handmaiden" (Luke 1:48).

Then, also, the willingness of Mary to accept the task that our heavenly Father had placed on her is a lesson in humility for us all. At times we recognize the true greatness that lies in humility. Some years ago, the members of a graduating class at Yale had a twenty-fifth anniversary reunion. As part of the festivities, they were asked to select the one person in that class who, over the past quarter century, had been most successful. In that class were included one person who had become President of the United States, two who had become U.S. Senators, four who were college presidents, and many who had risen to chief executive positions in business. But the person whom they selected as the most successful was none of these; he was a man who had become a physician and spent his medical career serving in a leper colony in Africa. Greatness can still be measured by humility.

And so the entire Church needs to recognize and celebrate the birthday of the Mother of our Lord for at least these three reasons: Here is provided a lesson in tenderness so often missing in religion; here is an insight into the workings and ways of God; and here is a valuable lesson in the meaning of humility.

God has chosen Mary. Both have chosen us.

Discussion Questions

1. Why has this feast been less controversial among Protestant congregations that observe some of the other feasts associated with Mary?

2. Does celebration of this feast make religion seem less harsh and judgmental and give it a more tender human orientation?

3. How are such virtues as humility and simple faith emphasized by the celebration of this feast?

4. Would you feel comfortable attending a Protestant service in which this feast was being emphasized?

15

✂ ✄ ✂

A Bone of Contention: The Assumption

The feast of the Assumption has sometimes been a bone of contention among those of Catholic and Protestant traditions, since the latter assume revelation comes only through one source — the Bible. Because no direct mention of this is made in documents of the New Testament, those of Protestant traditions feel they cannot accept any teachings about God taking the Blessed Virgin Mary directly into heaven. However, we do need to investigate this topic further before coming to any conclusions.

By the Assumption of Mary is meant that not only her soul but also her body was taken into heaven upon her death so that there was no long period of her sleeping, no grave as in the case with others, even great saints who wait for the last day for the resurrection of their bodies.

The feast, celebrated by the Church on August 15, dates from the fourth century, when numerous festivals honoring our Lady were common practice. As explained in Chapter 11, St. Germanus of Constantinople could write of Mary, "Her virginal body is entirely holy, entirely chaste, entirely the house of God." And, interestingly enough, the sixteenth-century Protestant reformer, Martin Luther, included this feast on a list of liturgical celebrations that should, in his words, "be observed among

Evangelical Catholics as a sign of continuity and order."

However, the Protestant community, while supporting many of Luther's recommendations, chose to take little heed of this one. Any recognition of the feast of the Assumption has all but been deleted from the liturgical calendar of most Protestant groups, if indeed it was ever included on most of them. While Protestants generally accept the assumption of Elijah (2 Kings 2:11) and that of the penitent thief (Luke 23:43), since both of these are directly mentioned in the Scriptures, they shy away from or even oppose suggestions that God also made it possible for Mary, Mother of our Lord, to be taken up to heaven to be with Him.

In opposing the tradition of the Assumption, they have failed to recognize what philosophers of religion understand as the two sources of knowledge: revelation and reason. While they support at least a limited view of revelation, they almost completely disallow the place of reason in the development of religious knowledge, doctrine, and practice.

The feast of the Assumption needs to be reconsidered in Protestant practice because it is based on sound reason.

Cardinal John Henry Newman makes four important points appealing to reason for the acceptance of the Assumption of our Lady.

First, he notes that Mary's Divine Son loved her too much to let her body remain in the grave.

The second argument Cardinal Newman advances is that since she was not only dear to our Lord as a mother is dear to a son but also was transcendently holy and so overflowing with grace that though she died for a brief time as did our Lord Himself; yet, like Him and by His almighty power, she was raised again from the grave.

The third argument is that ancient Church records contain no notes of a tomb of Mary. The early Church was very conscious of the tombs of the saints; for example, St. Mark speaks of the tomb of St. John the Baptist, St. Peter talks about he sepulchre of David, and great attention is given to the burial spots of Sts. Stephen, Mark, Barnabas, Peter, and Paul. If the Church was that concerned with burial spots of the saints, how much more would it be concerned with the body of the Mother of our Lord? Evidently, there was no permanent burial and therefore no body.

The fourth and final argument that the cardinal advances is that since other servants of God have been raised from the grave by the power of God, we can't suppose that our Lord would have granted that privilege to anyone else without also granting it to His own Mother.

Thus, the God-given power of reason should lead all of the world Christian community to the realization that the feast of the Assumption of the Blessed Virgin is based on a historical fact. The Assumption shares common elements with other Marian feasts of the Church, both in what it is not and also in what it is.

It is not, as some have accused, an attempt of a later Church to deify the Mother of our Lord and raise her to equal footing with Him. But the feast of the Assumption, like other Marian feasts, points us to the power of Christ, gives glory to the Holy Trinity, and becomes a unifying rather than divisive factor in the Christian community.

Devotion to Mary developed early in the Church, and some old manuscripts speak of the existence of philomarian groups. The Mother of God (or Theotokos) concept was formally introduced in Church discussion at the Council of Ephesus in 431. It was again upheld by the Council of Chalcedon in 451 and, by the end of the fifth century, Marian devotion had spread and led to the incorporation of Marian feasts into the liturgical calendar, among these being the feast of the Assumption.

In the life of our Lady, it is natural that her death should not be like that of other humans, since she was accorded a special honor. Mary died even as our Lord and Savior died, but through the merits of her Son, she also had been saved from the grave.

It is therefore fitting that she, body and soul, be taken to be with her Son and God in heaven. It is my hope that we Christians, Catholic and non-Catholic alike, will reconsider the importance of this event and gather together not only to remember Mary's death but to celebrate her Assumption.

Discussion Questions

1. Why was Luther so accepting of a feast that later met with so much opposition in Protestant circles?

2. Do Cardinal Newman's arguments in support of the Assumption make sense to you?

3. How can the Assumption be celebrated as another feast that ultimately glorifies Christ?

4. Would you feel comfortable inviting a Protestant friend to a celebration of this feast in your parish and then explaining to him or her the purpose of it?

16

☿ ♓ ♌

Rediscovering an Ancient Feast: The Immaculate Conception

Of all the feasts surrounding the life of the Blessed Mother of our Lord, none seems to be more divisive in the Christian community than the feast of the Immaculate Conception. Generally, Protestant arguments against celebrating it have been on the basis that it is not mentioned in the Gospels. To follow this train of thought, however, is to overlook the fact that many Church festivals are not specifically mentioned in the Scriptures but have evolved from Tradition. If we believe the Holy Spirit works in the Church not only through events limited to scriptural records but also in the ever-continuing medium of tradition and experience, then it is reasonable to believe that the celebration of a feast dating back to the eighth century ought to be taken seriously.

The feast of the Immaculate Conception commemorates the great truth that the Blessed Virgin was conceived in the womb of her mother, St. Anne, without original sin; grace came to her from the first moment of her being as it had been given to Eve. This does not imply that Mary did not owe her salvation to the death of her Son. "Just the contrary," wrote Cardinal John Henry Newman. "We say that she, of all mere children of Adam, is, in the truest sense, the fruit and the purchase of His

Passion." To understand Cardinal Newman's view and the stance of the Catholic Church on this subject, we must understand the nature of grace. God gives grace and regeneration at a point in our earthly existence. To Mary, He extended it from the beginning.

When the angel used the term "full of grace," it referred to more than a mere external acceptance of favor; it was, as the Church Fathers taught, an inward condition or quality of soul. While we recognize grace as coming to other Christian saints, it came at some time in their lives after birth; but in the case of the Blessed Virgin, it came from the first moment of her being.

Contrary to thought in some sectors of the Christian community, the dogma of the Immaculate Conception, formulated in 1854, does not ascribe divinity to Mary. She was included with the whole human race in Adam's sentence and redeemed by the sacrifice of her Son on the Cross, just like the rest of us. But the grace ascribed to her, so effectively presented by the dogma, is one of special recognition by God that sets the stage for the Incarnation of her Son, Jesus Christ.

St. Augustine in the third century explained it by saying, "All have sinned, except the Holy Virgin Mary, concerning whom for the honor of the Lord, I wished no question to be raised at all, when we are treating of sins."

Church historians point out that the doctrine of the Immaculate Conception was implied in the early history of the Church and never denied. In the Middle Ages, St. Bernard raised the question as to whether the Immaculate Conception referred to St. Anne, Mary's mother. The Church was again called upon to make its position clear, namely that the Immaculate Conception was not *of* St. Anne but rather *by* St. Anne in giving birth to the Blessed Mary.

We, as the children of Adam, are heirs to the consequences of his sin, that is, original sin. In this state of forfeiture and disinheritance, we are all conceived and born. But Mary never was in this state. She was, by eternal decree of God, exempt from it. It was decreed not that she should be *cleansed* from sin, but that she should, from the first moment of her being, be *preserved* from it. Those who assume the first position accord no special honor to the Mother of our Lord, other than that which is given to all Christian saints. Those who understand and believe the latter position give to Mary the honor the Church throughout history has sought to bestow on her.

With the papal dogma of 1854, the feast of the Immaculate Conception took on added significance. St. Anselm, bishop of Canterbury, appeared to foresee the coming of the proclamation when he wrote, "Virgin Mary, all nature is blessed in you." Writing in the twelfth century, some seven hundred years prior to the formal announcement of the dogma, he reflects that without the Son of God nothing could possibly exist, and without Mary's Son, nothing could be redeemed. The center of St. Anselm's thought is on creation in the sense that everything (as a result of the fruit of Mary's womb) is restored to original beauty. So he prays, "Lady, full and overflowing with grace, all creation receives new life from your abundance."

From all this we can appreciate the fact that the formal announcement of the dogma of the Immaculate Conception in the mid-nineteenth century was not a new idea suddenly designed to spark theological debate; rather it was the natural response to the flow of thought in the Church that existed for more than a millennium. It was also a recognition that the Holy Spirit continues to guide the Church through the ongoing medium of tradition and experience.

Thus, the ancient celebration of the feast of the Immaculate Conception ought to be an event for all Christians. In observing it we recognize its original intentions — to glorify God; to honor His Son; and to emphasize the reality of redemption.

Discussion Questions

1. Why is the feast of the Immaculate Conception one of the most divisive practices among Catholics and Protestants?

2. What do Protestants generally understand about what is meant by the Immaculate Conception?

3. How much importance is given to this feast in your parish?

4. Why was the papal dogma of 1854 just a natural progression of centuries of thought in the Church?

17

☙ ✖ ❧

The Rosary Is for Everyone

The splitting of Western Christianity in the sixteenth century, often referred to as the Reformation, resulted in the loss of some rich and meaningful traditions. For the Protestant world, one of these traditions that fell into disuse was the praying of the Rosary. This deletion from the devotional life was not so much based on any theological arguments against the Rosary but came simply as an emotional reaction against anything supported by the Catholic establishment.

Martin Luther prayed the Rosary as did other Protestant leaders, and nowhere in Luther's writings can we find him discouraging its use in devotions. However, as years passed, misconceptions and widening differences in practices among Christian groups contributed to its decline in Protestantism and its unwarranted reputation as being only a "Catholic" prayer.

In reality the Rosary is a prayer that belongs to all Christians. It is a biblical-based practice in the sense that while we pray the Rosary we meditate on the life of Jesus Christ. Rich May, Marian scholar and writer, sums it up so well when he says, "The Rosary is a story, a way of life, and a weapon." It is a story of the history of our salvation; the story of Jesus Christ, recalling the major events in His life — His birth, His childhood, His death, and His glorification. It is a way of life because it provides us with a model to follow. As we pray it daily, we begin to live the Gospel message it portrays, to live the life of Christ. It is a weapon because it is effective against sin and a meditation on the Word of God that St. Paul termed "the Sword of the Spirit."

Although controversy surrounds the origin of the Rosary, many historians believe that this popular prayer had its origin in the ninth century with a group of Irish monks who, as part of their prayer life, recited often the one hundred fifty Psalms of David. It was difficult for the laypeople to share in this devotion because of the length of the Psalms and so, encouraged by the monks, they instead said the Lord's Prayer one hundred fifty times in place of the Psalms. Soon after, the angelic salutation "Hail [Mary], full of grace, the Lord is with you!" (Luke 1:28) became popular among Christians in Europe. Thereafter, people began substituting the angelic salutation for some of the Psalms. In the thirteenth century, the practice of attaching particular meditation to each prayer (and later to a series of prayers) began to appear. When all one hundred fifty prayers were said, it was (and still is) called a "psalter." But a shorter form later developed using just fifty prayers that became known as a *rosarium* (Latin for "rose garden").

It wasn't until the fourteenth century that the prayer began to mature into its present form. The Carthusians, a group of Austrian monks, were probably most responsible for its development, grouping the angelic salutations into decades (ten each) with a Lord's Prayer between groups. (Another tradition credits St. Dominic, who lived from 1170 to 1221, with making the Rosary popular.) In the Rosary's present form, a meditation is usually recited prior to each decade. The older form known as a "scriptural Rosary" has regained popularity. In this format, a scriptural verse is recited for each prayer.

Archbishop Fulton Sheen helped us to understand this meaningful devotional practice when he wrote, "The Rosary relates the Christian life to that of Mary. The three great Mysteries of the Rosary — the Joyful, the Sorrowful, and the Glorious — are the brief description of earthly life contained in the Creed: birth, struggle, and victory. The Christian life is inseparable from the joys of birth and youth, the struggles of maturity against the passions and evil, and finally, the hope of glory in Heaven."

The Salve Regina, or Hail Holy Queen, portion of the Rosary was probably composed in the eleventh century by Herman the Lame, who was a monk of the monastery of Reichenau, a small island in Lake Constance (Switzerland). From birth he was lame and could not move without help. Herman, highly gifted and very pious, from early childhood showed a great love for the Mother of Jesus. At the age of eleven, his parents brought him to the Benedictine monastery of St. Gallen for his schooling. Later, he entered the monastery of Reichenau. He prayed the Salve Regina for the first time in the seclusion of that monastery. In this prayer he found consolation and strength in his bodily affliction. Considered one of the most prayerful and learned men of his time, he was a philosopher, poet, orator, musician, and theologian. He died in 1054, but this beautiful prayer has continued through the centuries as a moving appeal to the Mother of Jesus for her help and guidance.

Despite historical misunderstandings that have developed around it, the Rosary is not only a "Catholic" prayer but a beautiful devotional that needs to be revived among all Christian groups. Like so many of the Marian celebrations, its object is to bring us closer to the God who comes to us in Jesus Christ. In 1529, Luther wrote, "Mary is the Mother of Jesus and the Mother of us all. If Christ be ours and all that He has must be ours, then His Mother also must be ours."

Christian people should not allow misunderstandings of history to block their ways of seeking meaningful acts of devotion that are designed to bring them closer to God. A line in the prayer of the Liturgy of St. James reads, "Deliver us from all hatred and prejudice and whatever else may hinder us from union and concord." Such deliverance involves a reexamination of the spiritual values of the Rosary. Again, as the lay Catholic Marian writer Rich May puts it, "When we pray the Rosary, when we meditate on each Mystery — we do not see Mary, so much as we see Jesus, and we see Jesus in a very special and loving way. We see Him through the eyes of His Mother."

And so it should be the hope of Christians everywhere who desire greater unity in the Church, that we encourage the return of the Rosary to devotional life, recognizing that through Mary, we can come to Christ.

Discussion Questions

1. Why did recitation of the Rosary all but cease in Protestant churches?

2. Has the Rosary been helpful to you in your individual devotional life?

3. How can the Rosary become a meaningful way of relating religion to life?

4. Can a Presbyterian, as in the text, or any other Protestant, pray the Rosary without violating any of his religious beliefs?

5. Do you know of any non-Catholics who pray the Rosary or who might consider doing so?

6. Would you feel comfortable explaining the Rosary to a non-Catholic? If so, how would you justify its value?

Moving Toward the Future

Having looked at the ancient past and reviewed both practices and problems of the present, we are now in a position to turn our attention to the future. Using the background of Vatican II as a giant stride toward reconciliation of the divided Christian community, we also acknowledge the reality of a worldwide, international, and ecumenical movement toward honoring Mary.

The final entry attempts to bring preceding material together and to show why Mary is not a barrier but a bridge to greater Christian understanding, and hopefully someday . . . *unity.*

18

 ✑ ✂ ✎

Mary and the Church:
The Wisdom of Vatican II

As evidence mounts from events around the world of an increasing devotion to Mary, the resolutions adopted by the Second Vatican Council regarding Mary, the Church, and Redemption seem to take on a new dimension of importance. While Catholics, Orthodox, some Anglicans, and various other Christians have for centuries discovered the spiritual solace and strength that comes from seeking her help, the eighty-five participants in the Vatican II Synod dealing in this area had to be very careful in formulating a statement, given the new ecumenical spirit that was then in its embryo stage.

Traditional Protestant theology sees no biblical basis for praying to Mary for special blessings and expresses fears that veneration to her can slide into worship that is due to God alone. Protestants generally also reject the idea that human beings, Mary and the saints included, can contribute to human salvation.

Nevertheless, some Protestants are softening aspects of their hostility. An example of this is Church of England theologian John Macquarrie, who has proposed revisions of such dogmas as the Assumption of Mary into heaven that, he feels, can be seen as a symbol of the redemption awaiting all believers. Or consider the comments of Presbyterian theologian Donald Bloesch of the University of Dubuque, who says fellow conservative Protestants "need to see Mary as the pre-eminent saint and mother of the Church."

Similar and more numerous convergences are beginning to emerge as dialogue between Catholic and Protestant leaders continues to set the stage for mutual struggles to understand all aspects of faith.

As a backdrop to current discussion, the decisions of Vatican II, now some three decades past, still serve as a genuine meeting ground for the exchange of views and perspectives on faith. A document titled *De Beata Maria Virgine Matre Ecclesiae* became the focal point for understanding the relationship between Mary, the Church, and Redemption. Cardinal Ruffini Santos of Manila argued for a treatment of Mariology in its own right, that is, as a separate conciliar document, since he felt that to include Mary in a document that was mainly concerned with explaining the Church would be to reduce Mariology to ecclesiology. For Santos, Mariology was an extremely important consideration in its own right and should not be thought of as just a branch of ecclesiology. Such a reduction, he felt, should be avoided because Mariology is related to both Christology and ecclesiology as well. Cardinal Santos therefore argued for a separate document to avoid the error of either of two extremes — saying either too little or too much.

A reply to these thoughts was provided at the 1963 conclave by the archbishop of Vienna, Cardinal Franz Koenig, who favored including Mariology in the council's teaching on the Church. But he did not want to be seen as a supporter of an "ecclesiotypical" view of Mary, that is, a view that presents Mary as being only one Church member among others and, like the rest of us, passively receiving the benefits of the Redeemer. Cardinal Koenig wanted to present the Church as an instrument of redemption in the hand of Christ, cooperating with Him in the process of salvation. Then, he firmly believes, Mary may be presented as the one who, in his words, "in the most sublime way and as a result of His grace, cooperates with Christ in bringing about and expanding the work of salvation."

The day following the presentations of the two cardinals witnessed the casting of votes (October 29, 1963) by the assembly with 1,114 voting with Koenig to include Mary in the teachings on the Church and 1,074 voting with Santos to request the drafting of a separate document covering Mariology.

All this discussion and voting distilled down to a margin of less than two percent, which might well be regarded as a sharply divided house. But the figures are deceiving, for what really came out of this session was a deeply shared faith about Christ as well as the nature and results of justification. To the question of whether Mary is an agent with Christ or rather a passive beneficiary of redemption, the cardinals replied by making these three important points for consideration:

1. Mary's place is not with the Trinity but with the other recipients of her Son's redemption.

2. Not despite the fact but precisely because of

the fact that she is always one redeemed, she is like to community, which is the Church actively engaged in the work of redemption.

3. Because of the unique grace she has received, her role is of surpassing importance in God's plan of salvation.

Thus the Second Vatican Council was able to establish some guidelines for understanding the relationship of Mary to both the Church and to God's plan for human salvation. To appreciate the Mariology of Vatican II we must have recourse to both ecclesiology and to Christology. The council some three decades ago has presented modern ecumenical dialogues with a Mariology that is neither exclusively "Christotypical" nor "ecclesiotypical."

Those who engage in the search for ways to build bridges through better understanding now have an additional tool with which to work: Mary, Mother of God and mother of the Church, is associated both with Christ the Redeemer and also with us, the redeemed.

Discussion Questions

1. How can we justify devotional acts toward Mary even though they are not explicitly directed by Scripture?

2. Have you read or heard about statements being made by people who are non-Catholics relative to a need for greater recognition of Mary in Christian faith and practice?

3. Do the documents of Vatican II help to bridge the differences between the Protestant and Catholic worlds? Why or why not?

19

❧ ✻ ☙

Marian Revival:
A Worldwide Phenomenon

When her womb was touched by eternity twenty centuries ago, the Virgin Mary made a prediction: "All generations will call me blessed." The witness of the years that have passed since she made that statement forms an ever-increasing chorus to support the truth of her vision. Mary, the Mother of our Lord Jesus Christ, is the most celebrated woman who ever lived. The Jewish prophets alluded to her in their writings, the Islamic Koran praises her for her chastity and faith, while Catholic, Orthodox, and some Protestant Christians recognize her as the Mother of God, Queen of Heaven, and Seat of Wisdom.

In an age in which some would say that science challenges not only the biblical account of the Virgin Birth of Christ but also the entire story of divine creation, a grassroots revival of faith in Mary is taking place worldwide. Millions of worshipers of all ages are flocking to shrines, and there have been reports of sightings of Mary from Yugoslavia to Colorado and Georgia.

Interestingly enough, these reported apparitions sometimes embarrass clergy who have tended to play down such events and have been quite reluctant to encourage meetings concerning them. The Church hierarchy, according to Father Jacques

Fournier of Paris, are reflecting a skepticism about the populist wave of sightings.

In addition to this controversy, a theological tug-of-war is taking place over Mary's image. Feminists, liberals, and activists have stepped forward with new interpretations of the Virgin's life and work and, besides challenging the notion of her as a passive handmaid of God's will, are emphasizing her courage and individuality.

Regardless of whether she is viewed as a subdued handmaid or as an aggressive feminist, people around the world are traveling enormous distances to demonstrate in person their veneration of the Mother of our Lord. They are coming in such numbers that one national magazine referred to this phenomenon of the late twentieth century as "the age of the Marian pilgrimage."

Just to cite a few examples of what is happening:

✓ At Lourdes, which is the largest of France's 937 pilgrimage shrines, the annual attendance increased by ten percent over a two-year period to reach a figure of 5.5 million. The newly-opened doors of eastern European nations have contributed something to this, but it has also been noted that there is a significant number of young people in attendance, not just the aged and infirm.

✓ In Knock, Ireland, where fifteen people saw the Virgin in 1879, lines of the faithful have lengthened dramatically following a visit to the shrine by Pope John Paul II a century after Mary's appearance.

✓ At Fátima in Portugal, the shrine marking the

appearance of Mary before three children in 1917 draws a steady 4.5 million pilgrims a year.

✓ In Czestochowa, Poland, attendance at the shrine of the Black Madonna has increased to five million a year.

✓ In Emmitsburg, Maryland, attendance at the National Shrine Grotto of Our Lady of Lourdes has increased to half a million per year.

✓ In Medjugorje, Bosnia-Herzegovina (formerly part of Yugoslavia), more than ten million people had flocked to that mountain village since apparitions began in 1981 until the civil war put a stop to the pilgrimages.

To this impressive list there are countless less spectacular appearances that have attracted streams of the faithful. In the small town of Cuapa, Nicaragua, appearances have been reported of the Blessed Mother as well as at the Mother Cabrini Shrine near Denver, Colorado, and at parish churches in Colfax and in Santa Ana, California.

Now pilgrims and other believers are beginning to network their efforts. Some three hundred groups of Medjugorje believers now exist across the United States publishing at least thirty newsletters and holding a dozen conferences a year. There are seventy telephone hot lines that feature the Virgin's messages from Yugoslavia. In Alabama, one can dial MOM-MARY. Over the past several years, a Texas foundation has erected sixty-five hundred billboards inspired by Medjugorje.

Pope John Paul II can take satisfaction at this turn of events and simultaneously feel a sense of unease about it. While he has an intense personal devotion to Mary, he does not want to see commercialism take over the shrines nor to have her name used as a symbol for aggressive social and political movements. When he was made bishop in 1958, John Paul emblazoned a golden M on his coat of arms and chose as his motto "Totus tuus" (Latin for "Everything for you" or, literally, "All yours") referring to Mary. Once he put on St. Peter's ring he made Mary's unifying power a centerpiece of his papal arsenal. He has visited countless shrines and often invokes her in prayer.

In addition, Pope John Paul II is among thousands who believe Mary brought an end to communism throughout Europe, a feeling echoed by Father Robert Fox of the Fátima Shrine in Alexandria, South Dakota, when he says, "The world will recognize in due time that the defeat of communism came at the intercession of the Mother of Jesus."

While Church councils, theologians, and others will continue the debate over the validity of various apparitions and scores of other questions relating to them, it has become clear that the world is crying out for many things from Mary. Whether she is perceived as devoted mother or militant mover, as independent female or suffering parent, she remains the most compelling female figure in Western civilization. Renewed expressions of her vitality and relevance are signs indicating that people are still moved by her mystery and comforted by the notion of her caring. As journalist Richard Ostling noted, "Whatever aspect of Mary they choose to emphasize and embrace, those who seek her out surely find something only a holy mother can provide."

Discussion Questions

1. Why are more people around the world paying greater attention to Mary?

2. Are you aware of ways in which Mary's image is being used to support movements espoused by feminists and activists? Are these types of activities justified?

3. How should the average Church member view reports of apparitions?

4. In what ways do you see Mary as being a possible barrier to greater Christian unity? In what ways is she a bridge?

20

� ✻ ✻

Mary:
Bridge to Christian Unity

The agony that a mother experiences when her children are squabbling and fighting among themselves may be a fair analogy to describe the agony the Blessed Virgin Mary must experience amidst the quarrels dividing the disciples of her Son. In view of this it is not surprising that the bishop of Osnabrück in Germany has suggested that Mary be regarded as the "patroness" of ecumenism, the rallying point where Christians of all varieties may find unity, common goals, and mutual love.

A significant part of the divisiveness between Catholic and Protestant traditions has indeed been the place of the Virgin Mary in both faith and practice. Yet we must recognize that the split has been magnified beyond its real dimensions by misunderstandings on both sides, with Protestants accusing Catholics of using Mary to replace Christ and Catholics accusing Protestants of completely ignoring her position in Christian history. In the long run, both accusations are unfounded and serve only to further splinter the family of our Lord at a time when that family needs desperately to pull together.

If healing is to take place, both sides need to move beyond the point of party polemics and into the arena of honest dialogue. When this happens, we, the sons and daughters of one Lord and Savior, will begin to experience the reality of family.

While modern-day Protestants generally cringe at the suggestion of the Blessed Virgin as being a viable part of faith, this was, ironically enough, not a problem for the Protestant reformers. As Lutheran theologian Harding Meyer recently observed, "Luther, Melancthon, and Zwingli not only did not question teachings about Mary, they explicitly adopted them." These teachings included the Virgin Birth, the doctrine of the Theotokos, the *semper virgo* of the Fifth Ecumenical Council, and the sanctification of Mary as advocated by St. Bernard, St. Thomas Aquinas, and others. And even as practices of Marian piety and devotion emerged, with which they may have had some questions, they did not view them as problems of sufficient magnitude to divide the Church.

Having said this, we now recognize that the arguments about Mary, which have served to divide the Christian family, are not those that emerged from the concerns of the original reformers but rather from the petty bickering that has arisen since their time.

The job for both Catholics and Protestants in our day then becomes one of healing. We need to search diligently for ways of unburdening the Mariological problem that has so splintered our efforts at unity. These efforts are crucial when we realize that our divisiveness not only affects high-level theological discussions but also the everyday lives of the laity in areas as fundamental to life as marriage and the Eucharist. In all these efforts, the Blessed Mother of our Lord waits with open arms for her children to cease their quarrels and become a family again. She is truly the bridge to Christian unity.

The starting point for building such unity is the recognition by all that Jesus is our Savior and Lord. Mary, by God's decree, is always a part of that relationship. Jesus was, and is, God — perfectly human and perfectly divine. Mary, by never being divine, or even having been considered a deity, lends her person to being human in the same sense as you and I. She does not belong to Catholics and Orthodox alone. She belongs to all of us who profess her Son as Savior.

The Marian festivals of the early and medieval Church were Christ-centered, and the reformers wished to continue them. They viewed them as opportunities to focus on the Incarnation and not as some type of evil practice inconsistent with the Christian faith. These included the Purification of Mary (February 2; now called the Presentation of the Lord), the Annunciation (March 25), and the Visitation of Mary (originally July 2 but now May 31) as well as Advent and Christmas. Subsequently all but the last have been dropped from most Protestant observances and, with this, an opportunity to emphasize not only the central act of the Incarnation but also the role of the Blessed Virgin in salvation history.

Luther referred to Mary as "God's workshop" and went on to say, "As the Mother of God, she is raised above the whole of humankind" and "has no equal." Contrast this with the modern Protestant attitude that criticizes Marian devotion in the belief that it detracts from the central and unique place Christ occupies in human salvation and you begin to get a picture of the current crisis of division.

What Protestants have had difficulty understanding are the intentions of Catholic teachings about Mary. In the Immaculate Conception and the Assumption teachings it has not been the intention of the Catholic Church to elevate the Blessed Virgin Mary to deity status but rather to show her as the shining model of genuinely Christian hope. It is the hope for all humankind. Such a rereading and enlightened understanding on the part of the Protestant community will help to refocus the attention of the entire Christian world on Mary, not as a point of division, but as the real bridge to unity for us all.

Vatican II is slowly but steadily eroding the Protestant misconception that Catholics replace Christ with Mary as the world's Redeemer. Pope John Paul II, in a homily, said, "Mary's role is to make her Son shine, to lead to Him and to welcome Him." Such a statement can hardly be conceived of as some form of Mariolatry but as a genuine expression of a Christ-centered faith made more real by devotion to His Blessed Mother.

Another very crucial document to come out of the Second Vatican Council, the Decree on Ecumenism, underscores the centrality of Christ by stating, "The restoration of unity among all Christians is one of the principal concerns of the Second Vatican Council." This certainly says nothing about the Blessed Mother heading the Church, or replacing Christ or — for that matter — acting as an equal to Him."

What both Catholic and Protestant communities must overcome to accomplish what Harding Meyer calls an "unburdening" of the past is to refocus on the Blessed Virgin as a source of unity rather than division. The basis of this "fundamental consensus" is Mary as the Theotokos, or Mother of God, deserving of praise and devotion. Moving from this point, we can allow for the different practices of Marian faith and piety that appear in the Church and exhibit the flexibility that does not view such different practices as worthy of dividing Christ's "One Holy Catholic and Apostolic Church."

The Blessed Mother still opens her caring arms as only a mother can do to welcome all her children back into the one family, which is the Church.

Discussion Questions

1. Are you aware of any progress that is being made toward a better understanding of Mary between Catholics and Protestants?

2. Would forming a group in your own community, composed of clergy and laity, to study this topic be a worthwhile project?

3. How has divisiveness over the Virgin Mary developed more as an item of party bickering than one of real theological differences?

4. What can Catholics do to indicate that by devotion to Mary they are really honoring her Son?

5. How much variety in Marian devotion should exist in the Church?

6. Should many or all of the Marian feasts be regarded as optional in the worship life of parishioners? Or would this be surrendering too much of the real nitty-gritty of faith?

7. How would you explain to a non-Catholic that your devotion to Mary brings you closer both to her and to God?

Railway St

Foley St

Gardiner St Lwr

Seville Place

Sheriff St Lwr

Custom Hse Hbr

Amiens St

Sheriff St Upr

Beresford Place

ON TALL
MUSEUM

Guild St

Custom House Quay

13

Tara St

Moss St

Georges Quay

Sir John Rogerson's Quay

Samuel Beckett

Townsend St

Pearse St

Westland Row

Lombard St

Sandwith St

Cardiff Lane

**TRINITY
COLLEGE**

Pearse St

**NATIONAL MUSEUM OF
IRELAND**

Maken St

Grand Canal Quay

9

Kildare St

Merrion Sq

Merrion Sq North

8

GEORGIAN DUBLIN

Grand Canal St Lower

6 **15**

Merrion Row

21

Baggot St

Mount St Lower

Mount St Upper

7

Colin Murphy is the co-author of thirteen humorous books in the Feckin' series about aspects of Irish culture, along with the hugely successful *Stuff Irish People Love* and *More Stuff Irish People Love*. But he also has a serious side! He is the author of a critically acclaimed historical novel *Boycott*, about the 19th century County Mayo land agent who gave his name to the English language. He has also written two non-fiction books, *The Most Famous Irish People You've Never Heard Of* and *The Priest Hunters*, about bounty hunters who stalked Catholic priests in the 19th century. Formerly the Creative Director of one of Ireland's leading advertising agencies, he is now a full-time writer. His ambitions include climbing every mountain in Ireland and more importantly, visiting every pub in Ireland. He lives in Dublin with his wife, Gráinne, and their two children, Emmet and Ciara.

Donal O'Dea is the co-author and illustrator of thirteen humorous books in the Feckin' series about aspects of Irish culture along with the bestsellers *Stuff Irish People Love* and *More Stuff Irish People Love*, for which he is also the photographer—a man of many talents! Currently the Creative Director of Owens DDB, one of Ireland's leading advertising agencies, he somehow finds time to manage a children's football team, compete in grueling Alpine cycling challenges, play for a basketball team, go hillwalking, and do the gardening, not to mention squeezing in frequent visits to pubs to do 'research' for future book projects. Any excuse. Donal lives in Dublin with his wife, Karen, and their three children, Gavin, Leya and Alyson.

20 Things to Do in
DUBLIN
Before You Go for a
Feckin' Pint

Colin Murphy &
Donal O'Dea

FALL RIVER PRESS

New York

FALL RIVER PRESS

New York

An Imprint of Sterling Publishing
1166 Avenue of the Americas
New York, NY 10036

Text © 2014 by Colin Murphy, Donal O'Dea
Illustrations © 2014 by Donal O'Dea (except where otherwise credited on page 205)

This 2015 edition published by Fall River Press
by arrangement with The O'Brien Press.

For information about custom editions, special sales, and premium and
corporate purchases, please contact Sterling Special Sales at 800-805-5489
or specialsales@sterlingpublishing.com.

ISBN 978-1-4351-6141-2

Cover design by Elizabeth Lindy

Manufactured in China

2 4 6 8 10 9 7 5 3 1

www.sterlingpublishing.com

Contents · · · · · · · ·

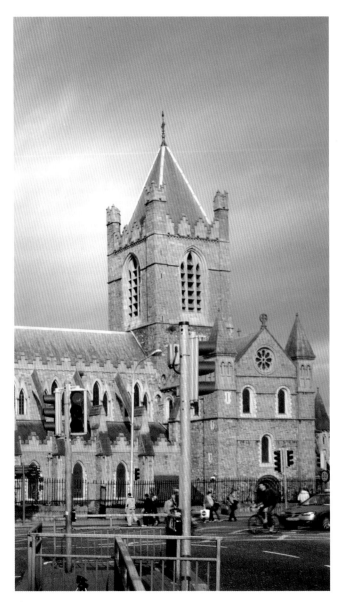

❶ Christ Church Cathedral

• • • • • • • • • • • • • • • • • • • •

Other sights nearby: *Dublinia, adjoins Cathedral. Temple Bar, 100m. Dublin Castle, 300m. St. Patrick's Cathedral, 400m.*

Here's the chance for a bit of spiritual sustenance before you begin drinking religiously. Well, ok, you don't have to be even remotely religious to enjoy a trip to Christ Church Cathedral, whose history dates back almost a thousand years. In fact, atheists, agnostics and even fruitcake scientologists will pass an agreeable hour or so here. It's got a ginormous spooky crypt, the theft of a guy's heart and even a mummified cat chasing a rat. What more could you ask for to whet your appetite?

♣ The History bit

Christ Church Cathedral was designed to be seen from the River Liffey, atop a hill overlooking the original settlement of Dublin. So naturally, Dublin City Council decided to build their Civic Offices right in front of it, virtually obliterating that view. But more of those gobshites anon.

The original church dates from 1028, when Sitric, the Viking king of Dublin, took a trip to Rome, where he clearly got some form of divine inspiration, either that or he had his arse kicked by the Pope, and hightailed it back to Dublin where he built the first, wooden, Christ Church. At the time this was the heart of the emerging city, and the Viking settlement was situated just below the slope on which the building sits, at Wood Quay. But in the seventies, and in the face of a massive campaign of protest, Dublin City Council decided to build their offices on the quay, which was among the most important archaeological sites in the country. That was bad enough, but the two concrete bunkers they put up were as revolting to the eye as a slapper's make-up.

Later they built another section of their offices in front of these, which was slightly less repulsive, and you get the feeling looking at them that they were designed to sort of hide the original embarrassing monstrosities. Anyway, that construction, along with the development of a four lane motorway on the south side of the Cathedral, virtually obliterated all that was left of the original medieval arrangement of narrow streets. Nice work, chaps. Gobdaws.

One of Ireland's most renowned saints, St Laurence O'Toole, laid the foundation stone to replace the wooden structure in the twelfth century. After he died in Normandy, his heart was preserved in a heart-shaped wooden box and returned to the church where it could be viewed until March 2012, when it was stolen, suspicion falling on rare artefact thieves. It puts a new twist on stealing someone's heart away.

King Henry II of England, who famously ordered the murder of Archbishop Thomas Becket in Canterbury Cathedral, attended the Christmas service in Christ Church in 1171—the first time he received communion after the murder, which made everything alright then.

Late in the century, Strongbow, one of the leaders of the Norman invasion of Ireland, would help to fund the completion of the Cathedral, for which he was rewarded with a tomb there after he'd kicked the bucket. The tomb was destroyed when the roof collapsed in the sixteenth century, and his remains were relocated, but the tomb effigy, which is in the church nave, is said to contain some of his organs, although which ones doesn't bear thinking about. There is a strange half figure adjoining the tomb, and legend goes that it is the tomb of his son, who he cut in half after he failed to show courage in battle. Lovely man. But like most legends, this is probably a half-truth.

The King who became a kitchen spit-turner

Christ Church once had its very own 'coronation' of a 'King' of England. In the late fifteenth century an Oxford priest called Richard Simon happened to notice that a pupil of his—Lambert Simnel, a baker's son, bore a strong resemblance to the Earl of Warwick, who was the same age and was a claimant to the throne of Henry VII. When Simon, who was part of a plot to place a Yorkist on the throne of England, heard that Warwick had died while imprisoned in the Tower of London, he started spreading rumours that Warwick had actually escaped and was under his guardianship. With support from the Yorkists, he fled to Ireland with Lambert Simnel and there presented the no-doubt bemused kid as the heir apparent to the effective leader of Ireland, the Earl of Kildare. Kildare either bought the story or was willing to go along as an excuse to get rid of King Henry, and so Simnel was crowned as King Edward VI in Christ Church Cathedral on 24 May 1487. Cheering Dubs outside celebrated the new 'King's' coronation. Kildare then raised an army with Yorkist allies in England and launched an attack on England, with Simnel as their figurehead, the kid most likely crapping in his long johns as he saw Henry's army approach. They clashed at the Battle of Stoke Field and Henry's army was victorious. Of the defeated, most lost their heads, although Kildare was pardoned, as Henry thought he might need him later to help rule Ireland. Simon escaped the axe because he was a priest, but spent the rest of his life in jail. Henry was merciful to Lambert Simnel, who he decided had just been a puppet in the Yorkist plot, so instead gave him a job in the royal kitchen. One minute he was a king, and the next he was turning a hog on a spit over a blazing fire. He probably considered himself lucky that he wasn't occupying the place of the hog.

Unfortunately, the head-the-balls who designed the original church had decided to put the foundations in a peat bog—oops. Surprise, surprise, almost the entire thing collapsed in 1562. Only the north wall of the original structure survived and it visibly leans—don't jump up and down if you're standing under it. The building stayed much like that for a few centuries until it was completely rebuilt in the nineteenth century. The church across the road was demolished and the Synod House erected there and the two were joined by an iconic arched walkway. As a result of all the demolition and rebuilding nobody knows which are the original bits and which are the new bits, so Michael Jackson would probably have felt at home there.

♣ Things to see

After you've had a quick look at the magnificent stonework in the church interior and a quick gawk at the tomb of Strongbow, head for the twelfth-century crypt, which is the oldest surviving structure in Dublin. At sixty-three metres, it is the longest crypt in Ireland or Britain, so it had plenty of room for lots of stiffs and loads of creepy tales. If it looks vaguely familiar that's because it was used for filming numerous scenes in 'The Tudors', although none of the nudie bits. You can actually hire it out for wedding receptions and Christmas parties, where some of the revellers will no doubt attempt to re-create a few of the X-rated scenes from the TV series when they get a little too pissed.

Eaten alive

Here's a chilling thought to ponder as you wander about the subterranean caverns of the crypt. There is a tale told, and with some substance, of an unfortunate British officer who was attending a funeral back in 1822. The officer—named as Lieutenant Blacker or Mercier by different sources—wandered away from the main body of mourners in the dimly lit crypt (possibly to have a pee), entered a large underground passage and couldn't find his way out. The passage door was subsequently locked and not opened again for—the accounts vary—either several days, weeks or months. To the horror of those opening the door, they found what was left of the Lieutenant—a skeleton picked clean and his sword still clutched in his hand. Around his remains were the skeletons of countless sewer rats, which the officer had felled before they'd finally swarmed over him, eating him alive. Yeuch. So, a word of warning—don't wander off down any dark passages.

Hmmm... I WONDER WHAT THERE IS FOR A MAN TO EAT HERE?

The crypt also displays stocks built in 1670 that used to reside outside in Christ Church Place, where you could be banged up for several days while Dubs threw rotten vegetables at you, if you were lucky, and the contents of their chamber pots if you weren't.

One of the most popular curiosities is the mummified cat and rat—nicknamed Tom & Jerry. It seems the cat chased the rat into an organ pipe sometime in the mid-nineteenth century and got stuck there, until repair work on the organ revealed their mummified bodies. The cat's pursuit of the rodent is now immortalised in a glass case.

♣ Go bats in the belfry

For a small extra fee you can take a guided tour up the eighty or so steps of a winding staircase to the belfry tower, and visitors can even have a shot at ringing the bells. Some of these brutes weigh over two tons—the bells, that is, not the visitors —and the circular arrangement of nineteen bells is a world record, apparently. You might like to know that these bells are traditionally used to ring in the New Year to hordes of absolutely gee-eyed Dubs staggering about on the street outside.

CHRIST CHURCH CATHEDRAL, Christ Church Place, Dublin 8
Tel:+353 (0)1 6778099 **Website:** www.christchurchdublin.ie
Admission and guided tours charged.
Location: Just 750m from Trinity College and 1km from O'Connell Street. **See map.**

② Dublinia

Other sights nearby: *Christc Church Cathedral, adjoins Dublinia. Temple Bar, 100m. Dublin Castle, 300m. St. Patrick's Cathedral, 400m.*

From the Cathedral you can make your way across the raised walkway to what used to be the Synod House, which now features the 'living history museum' called Dublinia. This is an extremely popular attraction, recently refurbished, that features re-creations of Viking and Medieval street scenes, including actors in full costume pretending to be ancient Dubliners. You can try and catch them out if you like, e.g., decapitate one with a sword and see if the others stay in character. Kidding.

HAS ANYONE SEEN MY HEAD?

There are three exhibitions—the Viking, Medieval and History Hunters, which looks at how archaeologists try to piece together priceless evidence before some moron city councillor decides to build a motorway over it. You can have fun dressing up in Viking clothes and be chained up as a slave, although maybe you're saving that up for when you get back to the privacy of your hotel room. Masochistic visitors can also try on a suit of armour—it weighs a feckin' ton. All in all, lots of innocent fun to be had experiencing this twenty-first-century version of life as it was a thousand years ago.

And if the steps in the Christ Church belfry didn't wear you out, there's another chance to go up in the world, as you may climb the ninety-six steps of St. Michael's Tower, which dates from the seventeenth century and, weather permitting (in your dreams), you can get a good panoramic view of Dublin from the top.

DUBLINIA, St. Michael's Hill, Christ Church, Dublin 8

Telephone:+353 (0) 1 6794611 **Website:** www.dublinia.ie

Admission fees charged (a combined ticket is available for Christ Church Cathedral and Dublinia).

Location: Dublinia adjoins Christ Church Cathedral, just 750m from Trinity College. **See map.**

③ Dublin Castle

• •

Other sights nearby: *Temple Bar, 50m. Christ Church Cathedral/Dublinia, 300m. Trinity College, 500m. St. Patrick's Cathedral, 600m.*

The first thing the visitor should be prepared for when they visit Dublin Castle is that it isn't, well, a castle. Not really. Ok, there are a few bits and pieces that look a bit like a medieval castle, like the roundy Record Tower in the Lower Yard, which is one of the only parts in which you might imagine a trapped princess being rescued by a knight, or something like that. But mostly it is a collection of Georgian buildings arranged around a cobblestoned square, the odd old church, a nice garden, and a few arched gate-

ways. Not to give the impression that it's not worth a visit, it definitely is. Just don't expect another version of The Tower of London or Stirling Castle. Anyway, let's move on to some interesting stuff.

♣ The History bit

Irish people have a sort of love/hate relationship with Dublin Castle. This is because it was the seat of British rule in Ireland for yonks, starting way back in the thirteenth century, but also the place where the British had to hand over power to Michael Collins in 1922 when Ireland won her independence—you can bet there was great craic in the pubs that night.

A river, the Poddle, runs under Dublin Castle. Well, it's more of a trickle, actually, and in most places it would barely cover your ankles. Yet its historic associations run deep, as the Poddle used to widen into a large, dark pool on the site of Dublin Castle gardens. The Vikings, who were the original settlers, called this 'Black Pool', which translates as 'Dubh Linn', which, you guessed it, evolved into 'Dublin'.

The only successful escape ever from the dastardly dungeons in Dublin Castle was that of the famous sixteenth-century rebel, Red Hugh O'Donnell, along with his companions Art and Henry O'Neill, who climbed down from a drain in the prison privy into the Poddle. So it was a sort of a piddle

followed by a Poddle. The three then escaped into Dublin's back streets and fled for the Wicklow Mountains to the south. Unfortunately, it was winter and they weren't exactly equipped with thermal underwear, having spent five years as a guest of the Brits. Art O'Neill died of exposure, but Red and Henry made it to the mountain hideout, although Red was minus two of his toes.

In the old days, the sobriquet 'Castle Catholic' meant that the Irish considered you to be on too friendly terms with the occupying forces of the crown. 'Castle Catholics' regularly had the shite kicked out of them.

In 1583, the Catholic Archbishop of Cashel, Dermot Hurley, was arrested (basically for being a Catholic minister) and imprisoned in the Castle for eight months, during which time he was tortured by having his feet boiled in oil. They sure did like a good old torture session back then. Then they hanged the bishop, for which act, by that time, he was most likely extremely grateful.

The first fatality of the 1916 Easter Rising was a Dublin Metropolitan Policeman called O'Brien. The unlucky fecker spotted about twenty members of the Citizen Army approaching the castle gates, and was shot when he tried to close them. The man who shot him was Captain Sean Connolly, who was himself the first fatality on the rebel side, shot while trying to raise a flag over City Hall, which is next to the castle.

♣ Location, location, location

Dublin Castle has been used as a location in countless movies and TV series, such as Stanley Kubrick's 'Barry Lyndon', Neil Jordan's 'Michael Collins' and Julian Jarrold's 'Becoming Jane'. Other less notable movies featuring the castle include the Jackie Chan action 'comedy' 'The Medallion' and the truly wojus, Irish-cliché-riddled 'Leap Year', whose makers are deserving of the fate of Bishop Hurley above. Still, thanks for the location fees, lads.

♣ Things to see

There's actually loads to see around the castle grounds, which cover eleven acres, including a number of museums, the State Apartments, an ancient church and the pretty gardens.

And the good news is that, except for the State Apartments, everything else is free. Well, not the cafes, but you can hardly hold that against them.

The **Chapel Royal** is worth a quick gander. The entrance is in the Lower Courtyard. It was built in the early nineteenth century in a Gothic Revival style, (in case you needed to know that to impress your friends). The interior is very opulent and ornate, with beautiful wooden vaulting, and the exterior features over ninety carved heads including St. Patrick, Jonathan Swift and Brian Boru, who kicked the Vikings' arses out of Ireland.

Down in the crypt of the Chapel Royal you'll find the **Revenue Museum**. Yes, there really is a museum to the guys who screw us for every cent in tax they can extract. But actually this is worth allotting a half-hour to as there is plenty of amusing and interesting stuff to see and do. You can take part in the interactive smuggling games or inspect a complete home-made still which is used to make poteen (a powerful illicit Irish spirit made from spuds). You can view a customs' toilet—specially made for inspecting the bowel movements of suspected smugglers. Bet you always wanted to see that! You can also see items that some unlucky customs officer

YOKE FOR EXTRACTING MONEY FROM IRISH PEOPLE

One for the books

The **Chester Beatty Library** is a must. As you enter Dublin Castle gardens, it's over on the right. Follow the signs. Now, it's not the sort of library where you can borrow a copy of '*Fifty Shades of Grey*' so you can read the dirty bits. And it's not just musty old books. Sir Alfred Chester Beatty spent his life wandering the world collecting loads of interesting historical bits and pieces, miniature paintings, manuscripts, and icons and, happily, left them all to us. A couple of years ago the Library won 'European Museum of the Year', which is like a Eurovision for museums, but without the brutal music. There are treasures galore, such as Egyptian papyrus texts or ancient illuminated copies of the Qur'an, and some of the items date back to the third millennia BC. And you don't have to pay a cent to see them.

extracted from the shite, like condoms filled with drugs, etc. Yummy. And there is much more to see here. Definitely put the Revenue Museum on your to-see list—if for no other reason than this—it is the only time in your life you'll deal with the taxman but won't have to part with any money. Yes, it's completely free and it won't tax your brain at all.

Next door to the chapel is the thirteenth-century **Norman Record Tower.** This is the bit that actually looks like a castle and it's the last intact medieval tower in Dublin. Nowadays it hosts the **Garda** (Irish Police) **Museum**, which records the interesting history of policing in Ireland, although unfortunately it as yet does not include any arrest warrants for the corrupt gougers responsible for bankrupting the state. It has lots of artefacts, photographs and documents including some from the likes of Sir Robert Peel, who was once Chief Secretary for Ireland and Prime Minister of the UK, and who gave the English police the nickname 'bobbies'. And unlike all the crooks that the Gardai have arrested down the years, the museum is free, although you have to call to arrange a visit. Number on page 25.

The beautiful **Great Courtyard** is where Michael Collins waved goodbye to seven hundred and fifty years of British rule/misrule when he accepted the handover of power in 1922. They actually shot the scene for the movie

'Michael Collins' on the very same spot. Long before that, there was once a kind of 'gladiatorial session' held here. To settle a dispute between Conor and Teigh of the O'Connor Clan in 1583, the authorities decided that they could turn the thing into a fun day out for all the family, and forced the two men, who were stripped to the waist and given a shield and sword each, to engage in a fight to the death. As the assembled officers, their wives and kids and various notable British aristo-crats watched, probably while munching on snacks of roasted sheep's brains and the like, the poor feckers had to hack away at each other until eventually Teigh chopped his relation's head off, which sort of ended it as a contest. Cue whoops of joy from the galleries. Beats a picnic at the seaside any day.

The tall thing on the north of the courtyard with the green dome is the **Bedford Tower** and the statues over the gates

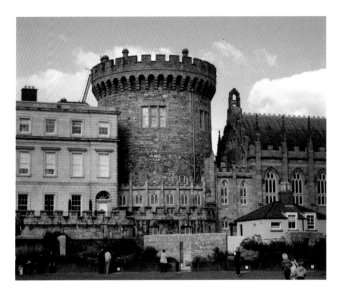

on either side are Fortitude and Justice. It was built back in 1761 and this was the original entrance; it had a drawbridge back in the day. The Irish Crown Jewels were mysteriously nicked from the tower in 1907.

The vanished jewels

The Irish Crown Jewels were stolen from the Bedford Tower in 1907. The widespread belief was that this was an inside job. A new safe was to be installed in a strongroom, but wouldn't fit through the doors. So the Officer of Arms, Arthur Vicars, suggested they temporarily lock the jewels in his office. Vicars used to get regularly rat-arsed and pass out, and on one occasion woke to discover he'd been adorned in the jewels by someone acting the maggot. Unfortunately, this didn't prompt him to increase security, so, when they went to fetch the jewels for the visit of King Edward Vll, they were mortified to discover that some sleeveen had done a runner with them. The king was reputedly like a mad yoke when he heard. The chief suspects were Vicars and Frank Shackleton, who was the brother of the famous Antarctic explorer Ernest, but both were exonerated, although suspicion about them lasted years. And the jewels? They were never found. Keep an eye out for them when you're wandering around the grounds, will you? The country could definitely use the dosh.

The **State Apartments** are basically a load of really posh, big rooms. They're beautifully decorated, of course, as they were originally the residence of the Viceregal Court and the place where the nobs used to hold their big balls. Whether you were a rising politician, businessman, socialite or even a rich young man/woman on the lookout for a bit of stuff, these were the parties to get invited to. Today they're used for such occasions as the inauguration of the President, and

for hosting state visits by foreign bigwigs. St Patrick's room is the grandest, and is where Queen Liz chowed down with the glitterati when she visited Ireland. Had she glanced up, she probably would have enjoyed the view—paintings of the coronation of George III, her great, great, great, great granddaddy, and King Henry II receiving the submission of the Irish Chieftains. There's also the Throne Room, complete with the throne where King George IV parked his bum in 1821. And you can even visit the state bedrooms and peek into the room where Maggie Thatcher slept with hubby Dennis in the early 1980s. What a wojus thought!

DUBLIN CASTLE, Dame Street, Dublin 2

Tel: 00 353 1 645 8813 **Website:** www.dublincastle.ie

Guided Tours of the State Apartments (including the

Medieval Undercroft) **are charged**.

Access to the **Chapel Royal** is free.

GARDA MUSEUM Admission is free and by prior arrangement.

Tel: 00 353 1 666 9998/9 **E-mail:** museum@garda.ie

Location: 500m from Trinity College and 800m from

 O'Connell Street. **See map.**

❹ St. Patrick's Cathedral

Other sights nearby: *Christ Church Cathedral/Dublinia, 400m. Temple Bar, 500m. Dublin Castle 600m.*

It seems there's no escaping Guinness when you're in Dublin, even when you're visiting one of the oldest churches in Ireland. Because it is largely thanks to another member of the famous family that St. Patrick's Cathedral hasn't crumbled and been replaced with a wojus shopping centre or something. But we'll get to that.

Besides having loads of interesting bits 'n' bobs to see, like most ancient churches, what sets St. Pat's apart in many respects is one of its deans, who happened to be Jonathan Swift, writer of, among other things, *Gulliver's Travels*. Many people think he was English, but no, he was a Dub. He's ours, so hands off! (Just like Oscar Wilde, who most people think was English as well.) So for anyone with even a vague interest in things literary, St. Pat's is one of the must-sees in Dublin. After all, it is the place where Gulliver's travels began.

♣ The History bit

The cathedral wasn't named after St. Patrick just for the craic, but because legend has it that on his early travels around Ireland, he began baptising us pagan Irish into Christianity at a well located beside the site. The river Poddle runs close by so there is definitely a source of water, but you wouldn't want to be baptised from it nowadays, unless you want dysentery.

Anyway, thanks to Paddy, a thirteenth-century archbishop, John Comyn, decided to make the church that once existed on the site into a cathedral, and a successor of his, Archbishop Luke, was mostly responsible for the construction, but unfortunately he went blind before it was completed, so he never got to see his life's work.

The building's spire, the highest in Ireland at forty-three metres, has literally had its ups and downs. In 1316 the original one (probably built by a distant ancestor of the guy who made a hames of your kitchen extension or your roof repairs) blew down in a storm. The tower was replaced in 1370. Unfortunately this one also collapsed after just twenty-four years. Worse, the damn thing fell towards the west end of the cathedral, demolishing most of it in the process. Finally they decided to fire 'Moron & Sons, Builders Providers'. The third version of the spire is still towering over us today. But just in case, don't hang around beneath it for too long. One last thing—the spire's clock dates from 1560 and was one of the first public clocks in Ireland. Luckily, nobody could read a clock at the time so you always had an excuse not to go home from the pub.

Chancing your arm

You'll see an ancient door suspended in a frame in the north transept. Funny place to put a door, you're thinking. But in the fifteenth century it was one of the main entrances. At the time, two warring families, the Butlers and the Fitzgeralds, were constantly kicking the shite out of each other and, after a skirmish near St. Pat's, the Butlers retreated into the building and claimed sanctuary. Eventually Gerald Fitzgerald decided it was time to bury the hatchet, and shouted to the Butlers that he wanted to make peace. Unfortunately, the Butlers suspected that he wanted to bury the hatchet in their heads and wouldn't come out. So Gerry hacked a hole in the door, telling his enemies that he was prepared, as a show of faith, to thrust his arm through the hole and shake hands. This he did, nervously expecting his forearm to be hacked off at any second, but, luckily, the Butlers' leader respected his act of courage and shook hands. The door has ever since been known as 'The Door of Reconciliation', and was responsible, it is said, for giving the English language the phrase 'chancing your arm', meaning to take a somewhat risky risk.

During the following century or so things went a bit topsy turvy, with St. Pat's being batted back and forth from being a Catholic church to Protestant and back again. After the English Reformation it was demoted to being a mere parish church and a Protestant one at that. Then Queen Mary, who was a Catholic, changed it back to a Catholic cathedral, and although you'd imagine this would have endeared her to the Irish, the fact that she also slaughtered a load of us during her reign sort of tarnished her image a bit. What a wagon! Then Queen Liz I, who we also didn't get along with, changed it back to a Protestant Cathedral. During Cromwell's reign of terror in Ireland the place fell into disrepair and the gouger held courts martial in the place. Cromwell is also said to have stabled his horses in the cathedral. In 1690, the Catholic King James decided to hold a Catholic mass here in advance of the Battle of the Boyne. Unfortunately for him, God must have been out to lunch as he had his arse kicked at the battle by William of Orange. William's right hand man, the Duke of Shomberg, cashed in his chips at the battle and William decided to honour him with a funeral at the cathedral—you can still see his tomb, and also the seat where William himself parked his arse. Another interesting tomb, and a deliciously gruesome memorial, is that of Lord Lisburne, who was killed at the Siege of Limerick. He was struck by a cannonball—use your imagination to complete the scene. The various bits of Lisburne were interred in the cathedral, with the actual cannonball dangling above him as an eternal reminder of the unpleasantness of his passing.

EH, MR LISBURNE?. CAN WE HAVE OUR BALL BACK?.

By the nineteenth century, the Cathedral was pretty banjaxed as there were no funds to maintain it. Meantime, the people of Ireland had made Benjamin Lee Guinness, Arthur Guinness's grandson, Ireland's richest man by enthusiastically quaffing as much of his product as they could get their hands on. So Ben decided to give something back by way of restoring the cathedral. It took five years and one hundred and fifty thousand pounds of Ben's money (about ninety million in today's earnings). Just think how many pints of

Guinness we drank so he could afford to be that generous. Not surprisingly, he is honoured with a statue in the grounds.

♣ Swift with the pen

How Ireland could use a satirist of Jonathan Swift's stature these days—the country is definitely not short of material. Swift was dean of St. Patrick's from 1713 until he died in 1745, aged seventy-eight, which was some feat at the time. Apparently he used to keep fit by running up the spire stairs. Fair play to him. He also had to remain fit to handle the women in his life. He had a famous relationship with Esther Johnson, who was the love of his life and who he nicknamed 'Stella'— her tomb is alongside his in the cathedral. They may or may not have tied the knot in secret (historians with little else to do are still debating this after three hundred years.) Despite his professed love for Stella, he'd also previously had a long-term relationship with a woman called Esther Vanhomrigh (he liked his Esthers). He nicknamed this Esther 'Vanessa'. But three's a crowd, as they say, and poor Vanessa got the boot.

When not flirting with his girlfriends, Swift took time out to write a book or two. You've heard of *Gulliver's Travels*, no doubt (full title: *Travels into Several Remote Nations of the World, in Four Parts. By Lemuel Gulliver, First a Surgeon, and then a Captain of Several Ships*), often described as the greatest work of satire in the English language. It has been made into about three million movies. But Swift was also a tireless worker for the poor, and gave away half his income to needy causes. There was so much demand from the poor for keepsake locks of his hair when he died that he was buried bald. He was awarded the Freedom of the City of Dublin for his efforts. His work with the poor also inspired a brilliant satire entitled 'A Modest Proposal', which suggested that the poor of Ireland could enrich themselves by selling their children as food to the rich: *'I have been assured . . . that a young healthy child well nursed is at a year old a most delicious nourishing and wholesome food.'* His satire didn't endear him to the very wealthy or the British Government, who tried and failed to shut him up. Naturally, he was admired in Ireland and regarded as a true patriot.

In his last years poor Swift went a bit wonky in the head. He used to pick quarrels with friends and yell at anyone who glanced sideways at him. He became wobbly on his feet and small noises could irritate him. At one point his left eye swelled to the size of an egg and it reputedly took five people to stop him ripping it out. Yeuck. He also went an entire year without saying a single word (now if only we could get Justin Bieber to do that).

He finally kicked the bucket in 1745 and was buried in the cathedral alongside his one true love (or rather, one of his true loves) Stella. Nearly a century later, Sir William Wilde, who was Oscar's daddy, exhumed his body. Why he did this is anyone's guess. However, he discovered that poor Swift had been suffering from Meniere's Disease. This can produce severe vertigo and small noises can seem like ginormous explosions of sound. Wouldn't you act a bit nuts if a buzzing bee sounded like an F15 flying around your living room firing weapons of mass destruction? The poor fecker.

Ironically, he left most of his fortune to found a hospital for the mentally ill, originally called St. Patrick's Hospital for Imbeciles. They dropped the 'imbeciles' bit, though. The hospital he founded still exists to this day.

♣ Things to see: Swift stuff

Swift's grave is marked by a diamond-shaped brass plaque at the west end of the cathedral, his epitaph on the wall above him. Right beside his grave is Stella's. And if you're interested in more death stuff, you can also see his death mask. If that still doesn't satisfy your morbid curiosity, there's a cast of his skull taken when he was dug up by Oscar Wilde's Da. A bust of the great man is set into a nearby wall. You can also see a bookcase displaying early editions of Swift's work and the original pulpit from which he frequently lectured Dublin's really rich people about the poverty in the city, sending the feckers home feeling guilty.

♣ Other stuff

The stained glass windows date from the nineteenth century restoration—and here's something you probably don't know —the way to read a stained glass window is from the bottom left hand corner up. At the west end is St. Patrick's window, telling his life story in thirty-nine images, from his kidnapping from Wales to his death.

THERE YOU GO LUV!

And here's a laugh. There's another stained glass window at the end of the south choir aisle commemorating Annie Lee Plunkett, the daughter of the aforementioned Benjamin Guinness. Well-known for her charitable work, the window bears the text

'I was thirsty and you gave me drink.' Jaysus, Guinness never miss a chance at some subtle advertising.

The thousand-year-old Celtic grave slabs discovered on the site in 1901 may be seen near the Patrick Street end of the building, close to the spire entrance.

St. Pat's also acts as a memorial to Ireland's war dead—on display in the North Transept is an original copy of the Roll of Honour, an illustrated list of the fifty thousand Irish men and women who died in WW1.

At the top of the nave (that's the main body of the church, in case you're wondering) is a pew that was reserved for the British royal family, identified by a carving of a lion and a unicorn. Among the bums that have graced this pew are those of Prince Albert, Queen Victoria and Edward Vl. Nowadays this is reserved for the President of Ireland, a fact indicated by the presence of a crest with a gold harp.

♣ The Lady Chapel

Behind the high altar is the small, but pretty Lady Chapel. A lot of cathedrals have these—a sort of church within a church, dedicated to the Blessed Virgin Mary.

This one was built in 1270. From the mid-seventeenth to the early nineteenth century it was known as The French Chapel, after those who worshipped there—a load of French Huguenots had fled to Ireland when their Catholic compatriots started chopping them into bits. Among the descendants of these French guys have been Nobel Prize–winning writer Samuel Beckett and former Irish Taoiseach (Prime Minister), Sean Lemass. The Lady Chapel has undergone an extensive restoration and features beautifully restored stonework and stained glass windows.

Holy crap

Ireland's first President, Douglas Hyde, died in 1949 and, being a Protestant, his service was in St. Pat's. Unfortunately, Ireland's Catholic Church at the time was so afraid of contamination by any other religion that they forbade Catholics from attending a Protestant service. Which meant that virtually the entire government couldn't attend the funeral service for the nation's President. Only one Cabinet Minister went along—Noel Browne—a man who was never afraid to take on the bigots. Even so, we had the ludicrous sight of the entire Cabinet hanging around outside the Cathedral until the coffin emerged, after which they were allowed to troop along behind it.

♣ The park

If you've had enough history and religion, take a break in the lovely little park next to the cathedral, called, you guessed it, 'St. Patrick's Park'. It's also the best place to get your pretty snaps of the building and, if it's a sunny day, to eat your sambos. This is probably where the original St. Patrick's Well was located. A literary parade of Ireland's great writers such as Swift, Mangan, Wilde, Shaw, Yeats, Synge, O'Casey, Joyce, Dillon, Behan, Beckett, and Clarke (we make literary geniuses by the dozen in Ireland) runs along the back wall.

ST. PATRICK'S CATHEDRAL, St Patrick's Close, Dublin 8
Tel: +353 (0)1 453-9472 **Website:** www.stpatrickscathedral.ie
Admission: The cathedral is free if you're attending daily service
(but that means you can't wander around looking at things).
At all other times there is a charge.
Location: Fairly central, 1km from Trinity College. **See map.**

❺ The Guinness Storehouse

 ·

Other sights nearby: *Christ Church Cathedral/Dublinia, 1km. Dublin Castle, 1.3km. St. Patrick's Cathedral, 1.3km.*

Considering that the Guinness Storehouse is reputedly the most popular visitor attraction in Dublin, you might imagine it should occupy pride of place in this guide, i.e., first. But when your book is called *20 Things to Do in Dublin Before You Go for a Feckin' Pint,* we could hardly start off by recommending that the first place you head for is a brewery.

Admittedly, there are certain things about Dublin that make it hard to avoid thinking about having a pint, like all the pubs, for one, or the Guinness Storehouse for another, it being a sort of temple to the great God, Boozius.

♣ Drink it all in

Now, there are two ways to approach the Storehouse, and we're not talking about directions on a map. One is to go there with your cynical hat on. The other is to leave your cynical hat in your hotel and convince yourself that you are off to experience some genuine history and cultural insight. Either way, what you'll probably end up with is a bit of both.

Let's do cynical first, because there is no denying that the Guinness Storehouse is possibly the world's single, largest, self-contained marketing extravaganza. By the time you've passed from the ground to the seventh floor your poor eyes will have been exposed to roughly the same number of Guinness logos as there are stars in the local galactic supercluster. In fact, when you enter the place, you are actually stepping into the bottom of the world's largest pint glass—which is a misnomer, as, were it filled with Guinness, it is claimed it would contain over fourteen million pints, almost enough to satisfy even a hen party from Blackpool. Naturally, Guinness

branding is ubiquitous as you ascend through the various levels—video displays, posters, logos of all sizes, pretty girls in T-shirts, etc. And in case you doubted that you were being exposed to a frenzy of marketing, there is even an 'Advertising Gallery', where you can experience what it was like for people in the old days to be brainwashed into buying alcohol. By the time you reach the Gravity Bar at the top, you will probably emerge from the lift like an automaton from a bad sci-fi movie, with vacant eyes, repeatedly muttering things like 'Guinness is good for me . . . Guinness is good for me.' And what's really ingenious is that you've been convinced to part with your own precious dosh for the privilege of being subjected to this orgy of advertising! You have to admire those Guinness marketing boys—they're some cute hoors, as we say. Oh, and by the way, make sure before you leave that you pop into the Guinness Store for some pricey advertising memorabilia. Yes! You are now going to buy a T-shirt, coaster, mirror, jug, bottle opener, snooker cue, ashtray, slippers, tie, golf ball, shopping bag, underpants or knickers, so that you can carry the Guinness message to the world. And besides, isn't it always handy to have a reminder when you're putting on your knickers that you should go for a Guinness at your earliest possible convenience?

Ok, ok, enough cynicism. Even if you found that all a bit hard to swallow, at least you won't the Guinness itself. So, ignoring all of the above, this place is a mecca for beer connoisseurs. (Purists will be apoplectic for describing Guinness as a mere 'beer', although Guinness themselves describe it as a beer, so Ha!) The brewery also occupies a fundamental place in the develop-ment of Dublin as a city and is a source of pride for Irish people, most of whom can expound on the product's attributes for so long you'll have grown facial hair by the time they've finished, and that's just if you're a girl. Well, Guinness is Ireland's most famous export—after people, that is—so what do you feckin' expect?

On your visit, you'll learn that this was once the largest brewery on the planet and still produces two-and-a-half million pints a day. You'll get to see a copy of the lease Arthur

Guinness originally signed for the lands, which was for nine thousand years, thus demonstrating supreme confidence in the longevity of his product. And then there's all the stuff about the building being in the style of the Chicago School of Architecture, in case you're interested, and also you'll get to experience age-old brewing traditions, the craft of coopering, where the water comes from, and the barges on the Liffey, and by the time you've heard all that, which, admittedly, is very interesting, you'll be gagging for a pint of the stuff.

♣ Pull a slow one

When you've reached the Perfect Pint Bar, a Guinness 'Ambassador' will teach you how not to make a bollox of pulling a pint, which you can then quaff and get your certificate saying that you, 'Fred Bloggs, has Poured a Perfect Pint', which you can frame and stick over your mantelpiece alongside the certificate for nude break dancing you got in Ibiza when you were nineteen.

Next up is the Dining Hall. And yes, you guessed it, half of the food is laced with Guinness, just in case you've managed to get this far without consuming any of the product—well, there's no escaping.

♣ They've raised the bar

Last but not least is the Gravity Bar, towering over the brewery, which has a 360-degree view of Dublin, and you get to enjoy a free pint, well, free that is if you forget the fact that you've already forked out a load of spondulicks to get in here. (There's the cynic sneaking back!). Anyway, it is definitely the high point of your visit (ha ha) as you can enjoy the world's finest beer while looking down on the poor eejits below working away to earn money to pay off Ireland's massive bank debt, which should be achieved around the same time the original lease on the brewery expires.

So, is the Guinness Storehouse worth a visit? As we say in Ireland: Is the Pope a Catholic?

GUINNESS STOREHOUSE, St James's Gate, Dublin 8

Tel: + 353 1 408 4800 **Fax:** + 353 1 408 4965

Website: www.guinness-storehouse.com

Admission Fees* *Please note that if you purchase any ticket which includes a free pint of Guinness, ID is required to prove that you are over 18. Under 18s receive a complimentary soft drink.

Location: The Guinness Storehouse is a 30-minute walk from Trinity College. **See map.**

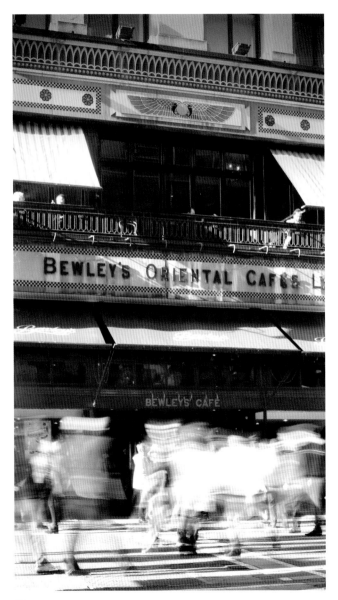

❻ Grafton Street

● ●

Other sights nearby: *Trinity College is at the northern end, St. Stephen's Green at the southern end.*

Right, time for some retail therapy, which is jargon for 'paying some international shopping chain loads of cash for vastly over-priced crap and then telling yourself you feel good about it.' Well, if that's what you're after, you've come to the right place, because Dublin's famous shopping street was, as recently as 2008, listed as the fifth most expensive shopping street in the world. So it's time to get your spondulicks out.

To be fair, Grafton Street has, happily, fallen out of the world's most expensive streets since then, and there is more to it than posh gobshites flashing ginormous branded shopping bags so that you know what rich bowsies they are, or pretend to be. If you're into that sort of thing, but are too broke/stingy to indulge in an orgy of over-priced shopping, a good suggestion is to go into one of the fashionable shops and buy the cheapest thing you can find, say a pair of jocks or knickers, for which purchase you will be rewarded with a nice bag bearing the shop's fancy logo. After that you're set. You can now go into all the cheapest shops where ordinary Dubs spend their money, and stuff all the jeans and blouses, etc. that were made in a sweatshop in India into your posh bag, thereby making you seem both cool and loaded while at the same time keeping enough money for the drinking you plan to do later. Ok, advice out of the way. Now you're ready to visit Grafton Street.

♣ The History bit

Grafton Street was named after Henry Fitzroy, the First Duke of Grafton, which is a tiny area in Northamptonshire in England. Henry was the product of a night of passion between King Charles II and his voluptuous mistress Barbara Villiers, so Grafton Street is named after a genuine bastard. He was barely out of nappies when his future bride was chosen for him and he was married when he was nine to a five-year-old girl, Isabella. Henry was made Duke of Grafton when he was twelve. After his father died and James II became king, he initially remained loyal, but then deserted the king to side with William of Orange in the Revolution of 1688. This would not have gone down well with Irish Catholics (ninety-five per cent of the population), but would have endeared him to the Protestants. His military duties took him Ireland and, after the Battle of the Boyne, he was sent to assist in the successful siege of Cork. It was less successful for Henry however, as a well-aimed Irish bullet put a large hole in him. His father had owned a tract of land in Dublin and the area was being developed at the time. Grafton Street was just a country lane, but was soon transformed into a fashionable residential street and named in honour of Henry. It would eventually develop into one of the most loved, and pricey, shopping streets in Ireland.

♣ Shopping, eating, drinking, relaxing and sightseeing. . . .

Yes, you can do all of that here, but by the time you get from Trinity College, at the northern end of the street, to Stephen's Green, at the southern end, you will probably have to take out a second mortgage on your gaff and sell your children into slavery to pay the credit card bill.

Starting at the Trinity end, this is the only section of the street that is not pedestrianised. The nice building behind the wall and railings on your left is the Trinity College Provost's House, but that's as good a view of it as you'll get, unless you somehow become provost of Trinity. Moving further along, on the right hand side of the street is the most photographed sculpture in Dublin, that of Molly Malone. Molly is a generously proportioned cailín famed through the folk song 'Molly Malone' (aka 'Cockles and Mussels') which has sort of become a Dublin anthem. It was erected in 1988 to celebrate Dublin's Millennium and in a flash was christened with several nicknames by Dublin wits. (See panel on page 46.) Whether Molly was a real person or fictional is a matter of debate, but both her fictional and supposedly real personas were street traders by day and 'Ladies of the Night' after dark. In short, she was a hooker. Here's the official justification for her prominent boobs: 'In seventeenth-century Dublin, women breastfed publicly so breasts were popped out all over the place.' Lucky seventeenth-century male Dubs.

Statue nicknames

Dubliners love to slag the crap out of new public statues by giving them amusing or smutty rhyming nicknames and often the same monument is blessed with four or five sobriquets. The practice began when a public sculpture was unveiled on O'Connell Street to celebrate the Dublin Millennium in 1988. This work, called Anna Livia, was supposed to personify the River Liffey and featured a woman lying in bubbling water. Within weeks some wag had nicknamed it 'The Floozie in the Jacuzzi', a 'floozie' being slang for a hooker. Not long afterwards, Anna Livia had a second nickname: 'The Hoor in the Sewer'. Eventually poor oul' 'Floozie' was relocated to Collins Barracks.

Anna Livia's spot in O'Connell Street was taken by the Spire of Dublin, which in a blink was re-christened 'The Stiletto in the Ghetto', 'The Stiffy in the Liffey' and most popularly 'The Erection at the Intersection.' By Jaysus, there was no stopping us now, and a statue featuring two old dears with shopping bags near the Ha'penny Bridge was named 'The Hags with the Bags'. One of James Joyce just off O'Connell Street was quickly dubbed 'The Prick with the Stick' and the colourful one of Oscar Wilde reclining on a rock in Merrion Square is called 'The Queer with the Leer', 'The Fag on the Crag' or 'The Quare in the Square.'

But in the nicknaming stakes, champion of champions has to be Molly Malone, the fishmonger famed in song. The Grafton Street bronze monument affords us a fine view of Molly's cleavage. According to the song, poor Molly died of a fever, but she might have died of embarrassment had she known she would one day be known variously as 'The Tart with the Cart', 'The Dolly with the Trolley', 'The Dish with the Fish', 'The Flirt in the Skirt' or 'The Trollop with the Scallops'!

Having taken a photo with your head next to Molly's boobs, cross over the Nassau Street/Suffolk Street junction and you're onto the pedestrianised part of Grafton Street, which runs all the way to St. Stephen's Green. There are a couple of banks strategically positioned close by so that you can withdraw a load of your hard earned dosh in preparation for putting it into the pockets of billionaire retail chain store owners.

Up ahead is the usual plethora of international fashion outlets, mobile phone stores, junk food outlets, jewellers, hair salons, etc. that you will find *ad nauseum* in most of the world's cities. British visitors may find some home comfort with the presence on the left, near the Trinity end of the street, of a Marks & Spencer. There's also a Disney Store on the right towards the Stephen's Green end. Luckily, there are also a couple of uniquely Irish institutions still in existence. The first you'll encounter on the right hand side, opposite Marks & Spencer, is Brown Thomas. The store has been around since 1848 and it caters for the poshest of us Dubs. If you can afford it, this is *the* place to shop in Dublin if you really want to make a statement that you're f**kin' loaded. If you're not f**kin' loaded, go in anyway and wander around with your mouth open, staring at the suits and dresses that cost the same as your car.

If you've emerged from Brown Thomas with any money left, you'll be glad to know that the next recommendation is very affordable and is one of the most popular and historic landmarks in Dublin: **Bewley's Oriental Café**. Don't let the 'oriental' thing put you off—you're not going to get any Egg Foo Yung in here. What you will get is a glorious cup of coffee, a lovely pastry, a nice atmosphere and lovely décor. This is a real café with genuine heritage, which is frequented by all walks of life. The company's been around since the mid-nineteenth century and the Grafton Street café opened in 1927. To the horror of Dubs its closure was announced in 2004, and there followed a campaign to re-open it, led by Dublin's Lord Mayor, which it did, completely restored, the following year.

You can also enjoy full meals in Bewley's—breakfast, lunch and dinner—and the dark wooden and glass interior gives the place a wonderful ambience. And keep a lookout for the beautiful stained glass windows inside, which were created in 1931 by arguably Ireland's greatest stained glass artist, Harry Clarke. Just don't accidentally put your elbow through one.

If you're in need of a bit of culture after the shopping, Bewley's also has a theatre, which hosts lunchtime dramas (and you get soup), and if you're there at night, it's also a venue for cabaret, jazz and comedy.

While you wend your merry way along Grafton Street, you will also be provided with free entertainment by a variety of buskers and street performers. Well, it is only completely free if you're too mean a bowsie to toss the performers a couple of coins. But especially at weekends, and during the summer months, the street resounds to the music of numerous competing musicians, along with mime artists, chalk artists and piss artists. It all lends the place a very nice, festive atmosphere.

Less than 100 metres further along from Duke Street, turn right towards Harry Street where, by day, you'll see a colourful display of flowers on sale by a number of street traders. If you're a man, this is an opportunity to buy your mot a bunch of flowers and soften her up before you break the news that you're taking her to a pub for the next three hours. Past the flower sellers on the right you'll see Bruxelles, a popular spot for generations of Dubs. It was also the venue where the band

Thin Lizzy played some of their early gigs, which explains the presence of a life-sized statue of the band's leader, Phil Lynott, standing outside. Phil was one of Ireland's rock music legends and achieved international acclaim with hits such as 'Whiskey in the Jar' and 'The Boys are Back in Town'. He died tragically young in 1986. Across the road you'll see McDaid's, a pub that was once Dublin's City Morgue.

Going the other way across Grafton Street will take you on to Anne Street South. The church you can see at the end of the street is St. Anne's, which is where Dubliner Bram Stoker, who wrote *Dracula*, was married in 1878 to Florence Balcome, a former girlfriend of Oscar Wilde's.

♣ The Gaiety Theatre

At the top of Grafton Street, at the Stephen's Green end, veer right and you will come to The Gaiety Theatre, which is regarded as 'the grand old lady of South King Street'. Almost one hundred and fifty years old, it features an attractive wrought iron and glass canopy over its entrance. If you're looking to experience the masterpiece plays of Irish literature, which you probably aren't, then this is probably not the place to come. And while it does occasionally feature serious plays, it is more the kind of place that puts on Riverdance performances, comedy dramas and pantomimes.

Handprints of some of the actors who performed there, along with famous visiting artistes such as Luciano Pavarotti, are immortalised in bronze on the pavement outside. Trivia: it was the venue for the 1971 Eurovision Song Contest!

♣ Off Grafton Street

The streets off the main shopping area also offer a multitude of delights in the form of famous pubs, eateries, more shopping opportunities and other stuff you might fancy.

The Powerscourt Town House (located at 59 South William Street) offers a quirky and enjoyable mix of shopping, history and dining. It combines one of Dublin's finest Georgian houses with a rear courtyard that is enclosed by glass, so you can enjoy al fresco dining even when it is pelting sheets of cold Irish rain. Even if you've had enough shopping, it is worth seeing the place. If you haven't, then the shops here offer an eclectic mix of arts and crafts, antiques, photography, plants, gourmet chocolate, etc. It's that sort of place. There are also a bunch of cafes vying to stuff you with all sorts of goodies and even a fancy pub which after dark turns into a place to dance the night away. You can also do tours of the magnificently restored Georgian townhouse and see what it was like to be really posh two centuries ago. To get there, retrace your steps to Brown Thomas and walk along Wicklow Street for 150 metres then swing left along William Street South for another 100 metres. The Powerscourt Centre entrance is on your left.

While you're in the neighbourhood, very close by is the **George's Street Arcade**, converted from a nineteenth-century market. This offers a more affordable alternative shopping experience to those that have squeezed you dry. If you've any money left, you can buy stuff here like vintage clothes, old coins, memorabilia, second-hand books, bohemian jewelry and you also have a choice of coffee shops and places to snack. There is a nice, casual atmosphere to the place and swanning around with a designer shopping bag will make you stand out like someone wearing clothes in a nudist colony. Only kidding. Everyone is welcome, pseudo-stylish people and all. To find it, walk down the street opposite the entrance to Powerscourt, called Castle Market. The rear entrance to the Arcade will be directly in front of you.

GRAFTON STREET, Dublin 2

Location: Facing the front of Trinity College, the northern end of Grafton Street is on your right. **See map.**

BEWLEY'S CAFÉ, 78-79 Grafton Street, Dublin 2.

Website: www.bewleys.com No reservations needed, but you may book a table online or by calling +353 1 672 7720.

POWERSCOURT CENTRE, 59 William Street South, Dublin 2

Tel:+353 (0)1 679-4144 **Website:** www.powerscourtcentre.ie If you would like to tour the Georgian Townhouse, call +353 86 806 5505.

GEORGE'S STREET ARCADE, South Gt George's Street, Dublin 2

Tel: +353 1 283 6077 **Website:** www.georgesstreetarcade.com

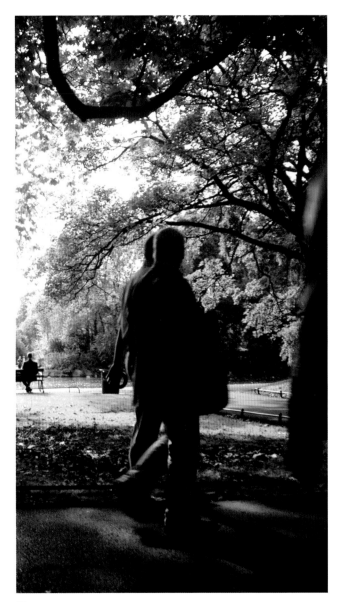

❼ St. Stephen's Green

• •

Other sights nearby: *Grafton Street, 20m from main/arched entrance. Trinity College is 500m away at other end of Grafton Street. National Museum of Ireland, 500m.*

By now, you may be suffering from what a crackpot shrink might call 'excursionist-associated anxiety disorder' or, as a Dubliner might put it, 'I've a pain in me bollox walking around looking at old buildings.' Don't worry, the condition can be treated very simply. All you need to do is grab a double mocha macchiato or whatever other phoney coffee-like crap takes your preference, and head for St. Stephen's Green, the place Dubs escape to in order to forget that their boss is a geebag, their pay is shite, their wife/husband is wojus in bed.

St. Stephen's Green is right in the heart of Dublin, at the top of Grafton Street—you can't miss it—it's the big green thing with all the trees. The park is roughly the shape of a postage stamp and covers twenty-two acres. But what lovely acres. The noise of the traffic seems to vanish almost as soon as you enter—the circumference of the park was planted with broad-leaved trees and a virtual wall of shrubs to achieve just that effect. Once inside, you can wander the flower-lined paths that snake around the pond, the statues and sculptures, the trees and shrubbery, the bandstands and fountains. If you're lucky you might even find an empty bench upon which you and your other half may nibble your Danish pastries, sip your coffee and watch the talent wander by. On a sunny day, you may also wish to join the others stretched out on the green areas, reading books, sunbathing or snogging, and getting damp patches and grass stains on the arse of their trousers or skirt. That's all you really need to know about the place. Relax. Chill. Look at the flowers. Listen to the gently sprinkling fountain.

But just in case you're afflicted with some masochistic desire to know more, we're here to please. In fact, St. Stephen's Green might be a nice place to sit reading this book, as it might give you a few insights into the place that would scare the crap out of most of the people in your field of vision . . . if only they knew what had happened on that spot. Read on . . .

♣ The History bit

Let's start with the leper colony. There used to be one here associated with a nearby church called St. Stephen's. But relax, that was way back in the thirteenth century. The area at the time was basically a big swampy bog and was also used as a common ground for grazing sheep. By the seventeenth century the City Assembly decided that the area be 'wholie kept for the use of the citizens and others to walke and take open aire'. A few years later, they realised they could make money out the place so they leased plots around the central area for building houses and made the stinking-rich owners of these palatial houses shell out a few bob on trees, forcing each of them to plant six sycamores around the perimeter, and thus we had the beginnings of the park. A wall was then built around the area and it became increasingly popular with Dubs. It actually became really really popular as a place of execution and of administering other punishments. Crowds would gather to observe some unfortunate gurrier being whipped, strangled, burnt, pilloried, stoned or hanged, though not all at the same time. (*See* panel 'Hang 'em high'.)

In the nineteenth century, the local householders decided they didn't want to have to smell the common riff raff above the scent of the flowers, which is understandable, so they made it a private garden in contravention of the law, but hey, they're rich, so they can do that sort of stuff, can't they? Naturally, the public were really miffed.

But thank God, once again, for Guinness, because in 1877 Lord Ardilaun, who was the wealthy great-grandson of Arthur Guinness, the brewery's founder, decided to buy the park and give it back to the city. What's more, he also paid for the landscaping, much of which remains today. St. Stephen's Green was officially re-opened on 27 July 1880. There were enormous crowds there to celebrate and police had to 'prevent velocipedes, vehicles and servants exercising horses entering the grounds'. *The Irish Times* reported that 'inconsiderate persons were seen climbing among the rockeries, damaging the place adorned for their enjoyment.' For 'inconsiderate persons' read 'yobbos'.

Hang 'em high

Until the late eighteenth century, most public executions took place in St. Stephen's Green, with roughly one execution every fortnight, and people would look forward to them the way people nowadays look forward to the next episode of their favourite soap. The criminal would be brought on a cart through the streets from Newgate prison, suffering the abuse of onlookers, and then, while he/she was still in the carriage, the rope around his/her neck would be thrown over a branch of the hanging tree and the carriage simply driven off, without its prisoner, who would be left dangling, to the cheers of crowds of happy, smiling Dubs. But if you had the misfortune to be a woman, it might not be so simple, as women were often sentenced to be burnt as well, while they were still half-alive from being throttled. In 1773, a Mrs Herring was convicted of doing in her hubby and her execution was described by a contemporary:

'She was placed on a stool something more than two feet high, and, a chain being placed under her arms, the rope round her neck was made fast to two spikes, which, being driven through a post against which she stood, when her devotions were ended, the stool was taken from under her, and she was soon strangled. When she had hung about fifteen minutes, the rope was burnt, and she sunk till the chain supported her, forcing her hands up to a level with her face, and the flame being furious, she was soon consumed. The crowd was so immensely great that it was a long time before the faggots could be placed for the execution.'

Now, there's something nice to ponder as you sip your latte.

The Green then stayed out of history's way for a few decades, being a sanctuary from the city. As it was put in a popular song from the early twentieth century:

Dublin can be heaven, with coffee at eleven
And a stroll on Stephen's Green
There's no need to hurry
There's no need to worry
You're a king and the lady's a queen . . .

Then, in the 1916 Easter Rising, the rebels used the Green as one of their bases of operation. Commandant Michael Mallin (later executed) was assigned to take over the park.

His second-in-command was Countess Constance Markievicz, an extremely rare occurrence of a woman being given a position of authority. Constance escaped execution due to her sex and would, a couple of years later, become the first woman ever elected to the British House of Commons. Mallin ordered his men to dig trenches near the entrances and the greenhouse was used as a first aid centre. But, after just a day, the British soldiers occupied the Shelbourne Hotel and began firing on the exposed rebels, forcing them to abandon the Green and take over the adjacent Royal College of Surgeons, which at least had a distinct advantage as a first aid station over a building made entirely of glass. Evidence of the gun battle can be seen in the main Grafton Street/Fusiliers' Arch entrance, where bullet holes are still visible.

An amusing aside to this event gives us an insight into the curious attitudes of the day: both sides agreed to a brief ceasefire so that the park groundsman could feed the ducks.

After that, the life of the park was pretty uneventful. The peace was shattered a couple of times by fanatical nationalists later in the century, but, luckily, nobody was hurt. The centre of the park was originally adorned with a towering equestrian statue of King George II, but poor old Georgie suffered the fate of many other ex-colonial statues when the IRA blew him up in 1937. He was soon to have company. A large statue of the Earl of Eglinton, whoever the hell he was, was also blown up in 1958. Nelson, towering above them all in O'Connell Street, must have been looking down and wondering how long before they got to him . . .

♣ Things to see in the park

The most popular entrance to St. Stephen's Green is through Fusiliers' Arch, at the southern end of Grafton Street. The arch was erected in 1907 to commemorate soldiers of the Royal Dublin Fusiliers who fought for the British Army in the Second Boer War. Irish nationalists hated Irishmen who chose to fight for Britain and the arch was nicknamed 'Traitors' Gate' at the time. It has become another popular place 'to meet the mot', i.e., the girlfriend.

Just through the arch on your left is a monument that definitely won't be blown up by nationalists. It was built to commemorate Jeremiah O'Donovan Rossa, a renowned leader of the Irish Republican Brotherhood, who was exiled to the USA for the last forty-five years of his life, but spent that

time raising funds to support rebellion and guerrilla attacks back in Ireland and Britain.

Moving past the monument and taking the path to your right takes you past the duck pond, where you might fancy throwing a few crumbs from your muffin to the over-fed ducks. Continuing on, a small, ornate bridge crosses the pond, and most people are unaware that this bridge is Dublin's second O'Connell Bridge. Across this you're into the ornamental centre of the park, which has two fountains and lots of pretty flowerbeds. Check out the interesting Blind Garden just to your right, which features scented plants that can withstand handling and which are labelled in Braille.

Just past that, hidden behind one of the so-called Swiss Shelters, you'll find an artistic installation by the world-renowned sculptor Henry Moore in honour of one of Ireland's greatest poets, W.B. Yeats. You'll know you've found it when you see a tall piece of metal that looks like it was retrieved from a train-wreck.

You'll also find numerous busts around the central area, including one to Countess Markievicz; the impressive cailín is depicted in the uniform she wore during the Rising. There is also a bust of Thomas Kettle, a remarkable barrister, journalist, orator and Home Rule politician who was tragically lost to Ireland in the Battle of the Somme in 1916, and who has no known grave.

Other sculptures around the park include a deserved one to Lord Ardilaun—he did pay for the whole place, after all. It is located on the west side, facing the Royal College of Surgeons. There is also an interesting sculpture at the south east or Leeson Street gate, which depicts The Three Fates—female beings who rule the destiny of man and the gods, much like your average marriage. The inscription in Irish, German and English tells you it was a gift from Germany for the help Ireland gave to German children in the aftermath of WW2. In the north east corner, the exit that leads to Merrion Row, you'll find a memorial to the more than one million victims of The Great Famine (1845–52). Walk around this and you'll see a monument to one of the founding fathers of Irish republicanism, Wolfe Tone. Given Dubliners' penchant for nicknaming their statues and monuments, it was probably inevitable that this one would become known as 'Tonehenge'—you'll get the joke when you see it. The location for the statue of Tone was chosen as it was directly opposite the place where he was born, so, naturally, some eejit granted permission for the building to be demolished.

♣ Around the Green

On the west side (the side the LUAS, or tram, stops) of the Green you'll spot the impressive façade of the Royal College of Surgeons. As previously mentioned, it was commandeered during the 1916 Rising and, like many other buildings of that era, it still carries bullet holes in its façade. Moving along towards Grafton Street you will see the St. Stephen's Green Shopping Centre, which was designed to look like a conservatory. Opened in 1988, at the time it was the largest in Ireland, but since then we've built a shopping centre for approximately every six people in the country. The anchor tenant is Dunnes Stores, Ireland's ubiquitous and oldest supermarket/clothes retailer. You'll find the stuff in there a good bit cheaper than Grafton Street. Music fans may wish to note that the centre was built on the site of the Dandelion Market, where U2 performed their first gigs to an audience of about fifty people in the 1970s.

♣ The Little Museum of Dublin

Turn right along the north side of the Green and a couple of hundred metres along you'll see the charming Little Museum of Dublin, located in a beautiful Georgian building and featuring twentieth-century memorabilia, all of which have been donated by the public. Here you'll see stuff like posters of U2's early gigs, product packaging from the 1900s, a first edition of James Joyce's *Ulysses* and something that is even more rare and priceless—a Ryanair *Business Class* ticket! It's worth taking the guided tour.

Further along the north side you'll see what is possibly Ireland's most famous hotel, the Shelbourne. Despite the owners remaining loyal to the crown during the Rising, when British soldiers occupied the building, the nationalist

porter regularly sneaked on to the roof to signal the British troop movements. During the fighting, the hotel also took in wounded from both sides, some being treated by the well-to-do lady guests. In 1922, the Irish Constitution was drafted in room 112. Among the Shelbourne's guests down the years have been Stan Laurel, Oliver Hardy, James Cagney, John Wayne, Maureen O'Hara, Orson Wells, Elizabeth Taylor, Richard Burton, Rita Hayworth, and John F. Kennedy and the missus, Jackie. The famous Horseshoe Bar even merited a mention in James Joyce's *Ulysses*. Oh, and Hitler's half brother, Alois Hitler, worked as a waiter in the Shelbourne.

ST. STEPHEN'S GREEN, Dublin 2

Tel: +353 1 475 7816, **Email:** info@heritageireland.ie

No entrance fee.

LITTLE MUSEUM OF DUBLIN, 15 St Stephen's Green.

Tel: 353 1 6611000, **Website:** www.littlemuseum.ie

Entrance fees charged.

Location: The Green is at the southern end of Grafton Street.

See map.

⑧ Georgian Dublin

• •

Other sights nearby: *From NW corner of Merrion Square: Grafton Street, 600m, Trinity College, 700m.*

Time to get street smart and see a bit of Dublin's great architectural heritage and also to work up a thirst for later. You may have spotted one or two of Dublin's Georgian buildings in your wanderings so far—they're mainly the red brick ones with the colourful doorways. They used to be the townhouses of upwardly mobile types of the eighteenth century. They were also the homes of loads of famous people you've probably heard of and you can spot a few of these as we move along. While some of Dublin's Georgian architecture has been demolished and replaced with structures so ugly they make a wart on a bulldog's face seem beautiful, many of the streetscapes are virtually untouched by the march of 'progress'. So let's take a stroll back to the days of cobbled streets, fine gentlemen with tops hats and elegant ladies with hooped dresses.

♣ The History bit

The eighteenth century saw the development in Dublin of architecture that was almost all of the same style, called Palladian. Unfortunately poor Palladio, who created it, was a dead Italian Catholic, so they definitely weren't going to name the style after him. This was during the reigns of Kings George I through IV. You guessed it: it was named the Georgian style.

A body called the Wide Streets Commission was formed to get rid of many of the tumbledown ancient dwellings and as a result we got streets such as O'Connell Street and Dame Street. On the north side of the Liffey two major squares were built, Mountjoy Square and Parnell Square, each a central park surrounded by elegant residential homes, and these became the trendy places to live for the hoity toity. It should be pointed out that the hoity toity at the time were almost all Protestants, so the only time a Catholic saw the inside of one of these homes was when he or she was delivering the coal or working there cleaning out its jacks.

Anyway, one day Ireland's most senior peer, the Duke of Leinster, decided to build himself a new home on the south-side that would really distinguish him from the common or garden millionaires, and the result was Leinster House, now the seat of the Irish Parliament—at the time it was regarded as a country mansion.

Of course all the other toffs followed him like rats after the pied piper, with the result that the northside squares gradually fell into disrepair and were eventually rented out to Catholic families—an entire family got a room to share. Inevitably the buildings deteriorated into overcrowded slums. Mountjoy Square in particular never really recovered and despite the tireless efforts of the people who live there now, it is, shamefully, the most neglected of Dublin's Georgian Squares, although it has recently been designated an Architectural Conservation Area.

Northside-Southside

It is ironic that in the early days of modern Dublin the northside was the posh/trendy place, as nowadays the northside is the butt of lots of slagging and jokes from southside Dubs, the southsiders considering themselves to be the posh, sophisticated ones. This northside/southside slagging is generally good natured and takes the form of jokes such as:

Q: What do you call a northsider at Trinity College?

A: The doorman.

Q: What do northsiders use for protection when they're having sex?

A: A bus shelter.

Naturally the northsiders have hit back by poking fun at the notion that southsiders are a lazy lot who live off their parents and wouldn't know a day's hard work if it kicked them in the arse.

Q: What does a southsider say on his first day at work?

A: What do I do now, Daddy?

But the one that best sums up the northside/southside thing is this:

Q: What's the difference between northside girls and southside girls?

A: Northside girls have fake jewellery and real orgasms.

Meantime, new squares and streets were springing up all over southside Dublin, which became the new trendy quarter. Merrion Square was the most elegant, followed by the smaller Fitzwilliam Square. An extensive network of streets snaked out from these squares and by the early nineteenth century, Dublin's southside had a large network of beautiful Georgian streets. Up until the 1960s the area had the longest Georgian streetscape in the world, and then the Electricity Supply Board demolished a bunch of the houses and threw up a hideous lump of a building slap bang in the middle. Actually, as you explore you'll find that most of the former homes are now offices to lawyers, internet companies, ad agencies and accountants. But at least they're not abandoned.

♣ Take a walk, pal

There are lots of walking tours you can go on if you'd like to see Georgian Dublin up close. A number of them are listed below. But here's a short DIY guide, which will save you a few bob. This walk will only take you about an hour. Right, walking shoes on, let's get started.

Have a look at the map. We're heading for Merrion Square, and it's easy to find. Facing the front entrance to Trinity College, turn right and follow the wall of the college into Nassau Street for about 600 metres until the road forks. Continue directly ahead into Clare Street (itself lined with pretty Georgian buildings) for another 100 metres, which will take you to our starting point.

You are standing on the corner of Merrion Square, one of the best-preserved in Dublin. There was a plan in the 1920s to wipe Merrion Square off the map and build a cathedral here. Luckily, attitudes have long since changed and strict building and planning guidelines now protect what remains of our Georgian heritage. And one of the great things about Georgian Dublin was the level of planning and building control that went on at the time. Every building had to conform to certain specifications and the streets were purposely built to accommodate traffic and not to give a sense of overcrowding.

Right across the road on the corner you'll see a building called the American College. This is No. 1 Merrion Square and was the very first of the homes built here—it also has quite a claim to fame in that it was the home where Oscar Wilde grew up. The first two floors have been beautifully restored to the way they would have appeared in Oscar's day, but unfortunately you can only visit them as part of a group tour. So unless you've got twenty-four people with you and have made an advance booking, tough. Never mind, you'll have the opportunity to see the inside of another real Georgian home later. But for now, let's meet the great Oscar himself, or at least a quirky version of him. Turn right into the square and cross the road to the park. About half way along you'll come to a gate. But take a moment to look across the road. That's the front of the **National Gallery of Ireland** on the right and on its left is the back of Leinster House. Well, actually, this is the original front of the building with its nice lawns and monuments. But not knowing the front from the back sits very well with Irish politicians, who never know whether they're coming or going.

And if you fancy a bit of mental stimulation, **The National Gallery** is well worth a visit in its own right. It houses the national collection of Irish and European art and includes works by lots of really big dudes in the art world like Monet, Goya, Picasso, Van Gogh, Rembrandt, Caravaggio, etc. as well as the National Portrait Collection. There are regular exhibitions including an annual January exhibiton of Turner's watercolours. You can also take a tour of the highlights of the collection.

Ok, turn into the park. That pyramid-shaped monument in front of you is a memorial to all of the members of the Irish defence forces who have died in service and features

an eternal flame guarded by four sentries. It is one of many monuments in the park.

Turn left and follow the railings to the corner of the park, where you'll find the sculpture of Oscar Wilde. This is not your average sculpture, to say the least. It shows Oscar reclining on a granite boulder facing his old gaff. His seemingly uncomfortable position no doubt accounts for his expression—half grimace, half smile. His colourful clothes are made of precious stones including jade and pink thulite. The pregnant mot in the nip and the male torso nearby are said to represent Oscar's ambiguous sexual preferences, so make of that what you will. But it does explain the nicknames that Dubs have given the sculpture, e.g. 'The Fag on the Crag' (see panel 'Statue Nicknames', page 46).

After you've done that, let's take a walk around the square itself. Go back out the gate you came through and turn right back toward Oscar's house. Right again and follow the line of the houses on the left. The doorways of these buildings have become something of an icon of Dublin—there's a famous poster called 'The Doors of Dublin' that has been around for yonks. Some of the doors are brightly painted, with the curved fanlight above and often with floral arrangements around them. Because the regulations regarding the original buildings had to be so strictly adhered to, the doorways were one of the few opportunities that owners had to make an individual statement about their home, like 'I'm stinking rich.' Also keep an eye out for the circular metal plates you might spot in the ground here and there. These were the 'coal holes'—where the coal was delivered to the house so that the wealthy bowsies upstairs wouldn't have to get their hands dirty and the poor eejit in the basement could collect it in buckets and haul it up to the upper floors.

Carry on until you come to the corner of the park. The big building on the left is the National Maternity Hospital, which could come in handy if you happen to go into labour at precisely this moment. Turn right on to the east side of the square. The building at No. 39 used to house the British Embassy, that was until the Bloody Sunday massacre in Northern Ireland in 1972 sparked huge protests and a mob shamefully burned the embassy to the ground. But on to lighter matters.

When you reach the next corner you'll have the opportunity to experience what it was like to live in one of these beautiful residences back in the days when the street you're standing in was covered with horseshite. Directly opposite, on the corner of Fitzwilliam Street Lower and Mount Street Upper is No. 29, the **Georgian House Museum**. This is one of the best little museums in Dublin and you can enjoy a sort of do-it-yourself tour where you simply wander around the house, or else take one of the official guided tours. Inside you'll get a real sense of the 'upstairs-downstairs' lives of the people who lived here, i.e., where they and their servants ate, drank, entertained, dossed around, slept and dressed. It is complete with all the furnishings and decorations of the time and still features the original interiors. If you've any interest at all in the past, or at least in how posh people lived in the past, don't miss it.

Ok, that done, on the way out of No. 29 there's a nice little photo op as you look along the length of Mount Street Upper, which is lined with more Georgian buildings. The cute church at the end of the street is St. Stephen's, but hardly anyone in Dublin could tell you that, as everyone calls it The Pepper Canister. Guess why?

BTW, music fans may recognise these streets from the video of U2's 'The Sweetest Thing', which featured, among other things, an elephant and male strippers on top of a fire brigade following Bono as he drove down the street.

Continue along Merrion Square South. At No. 58 you'll see the house where Daniel O'Connell lived (he of O'Connell Street), known as The Liberator. Dan the Man didn't liberate us from Britain, but from religious persecution. He was a pacifist, but you may be interested to know that he only became one after blowing some guy away in a duel.

No. 65 was once the workplace of one Erwin Schrödinger, Nobel Prize–winning founder of Wave Mechanics. He did a lot of his deep thinking here and came up with the famous Schrödinger Equation. You'll need to learn this off so you can discuss it in the pub later:

$$-e^{-\frac{iEt}{\hbar}} \frac{\hbar^2}{2m_0} \frac{d^2\psi(x)}{d^2} + e^{-\frac{iEt}{\hbar}} U(x)\,\psi(x) = i\hbar\,\frac{-iEt}{\hbar}\,\psi(x)e^{-\frac{iEt}{\hbar}}$$

Got that? Great. Moving along, No. 70 was once the home of Sheridan Le Fanu, who, in case you didn't know, was the leading ghost story writer of the Victorian era.

You'll find the former gaff of our legendary Nobel Prize–winning poet W.B. Yeats at No. 82. He was one of the greatest literary figures in the twentieth century and just so you can bluff that you're a literary type, here's a line or two of his poetry to learn off:

But I, being poor, have only my dreams;
I have spread my dreams under your feet;
Tread softly because you tread on my dreams.

So, continuing to tread softly past Mr. Yeats's place, a couple of doors down at No. 84 was once the workplace of renowned Irish nationalist writer and painter George William Russell, also known as Æ (A.E.). Old A.E. was considered a mystical writer and painter and he believed himself to be clairvoyant, so he could read your thoughts. You filthy thing. Wait until you get back to the hotel!

You've now gone full circle, or square, and you're going to take a left turn into Merrion Row. Pubs coming. Lots of them.

The building on your left that is now the Merrion Hotel was once the home of the Duke of Wellington, and the big white yoke on the right is Government Buildings, which was opened by King George V in 1911 and whose architect, Aston Webb, also designed the façade of Buckingham Palace.

You have now reached the junction of Baggot Street Lower to your left, and Merrion Row on your right. At this point you might just be in need of a bit of liquid relaxation. And luckily there are plenty of pubs in either direction. Decisions, decisions. (See Dublin Pubs on page 170 for individual commentary).

Heading left you'll encounter Doheny & Nesbitt on your left and Toners on your right. Further along, if you take a brief right along Pembroke Row you'll see The Pembroke, where Michelle Obama and the kids and about three hundred security guys had their lunch while in Dublin. Incidentally, if you continue along Pembroke Row for a bit, you will emerge into a mini-Merrion Square, called Fitzwilliam Square.

Retrace your steps right back to Merrion Row and continue along, where you'll find the famous O'Donoghue's Pub, the cradle of many a trad music legend. There are also lots of restaurants and coffee shops in Baggot Street/Merrion Row.

But just to finish our tour, continue along Merrion Row and you'll come to St. Stephen's Green. Just at the end of the street on the right is a tiny little cemetery hidden away in a corner. The graves here belong to French Huguenots who fled persecution in France in the 1600s. You can't enter it but you can see a list of those buried here on the wall, one of whom is a Becquett, who was an ancestor of Samuel, yet another one of our Nobel Prize–winning writers. We just churn 'em out.

Been nice walking with you.

OSCAR WILDE HOUSE, No. 1 Merrion Square, Dublin 2

Tel: +353 (0)1 662 0281

Website: www.amcd.ie/about-us/history/oscar-wilde-house

NUMBER 29, The Georgian House Museum, 29 Fitzwilliam Street Lower, Dublin 2

Tel: +353 (0)1-702 6165

Website: www.esb.ie/no29

Morning tours reserved for groups, and must be pre-booked.

Afternoon tours on a first-come first-served basis.

Admission charged.

THE NATIONAL GALLERY OF IRELAND, Merrion Square West, Dublin 2

Tel: +353 1 661 5133

Website: www.nationalgallery.ie

Admission is free.

WALKING TOURS:

- Dublin Tourism's iWalks—free podcast audio guides to Dublin.
  Contact Dublin Tourism Centre, Suffolk Street.
  Tel: + 1850 230 330 **Web:** www.visitdublin.com/iwalks
- Pat Liddy's Walking Tours
  Tel: +353 (0)1 8329 406 **Website:** www.walkingtours.ie
- Historical Walking Tours of Dublin
  Tel: +353 (0)87 6889412
  Website: historicaltours.ie

Location: Merrion Square is approximately 800m from Trinity College main entrance. **See map.**

⑨ The National Museum of Ireland

. . . .

Other sights nearby: *St. Stephen's Green, nearest entrance 150m, Grafton Street, 350m.*

Did you know that while the ancient Egyptians were still living in caves and incapable of building a sandcastle, never mind a pyramid, the Irish were building tombs so accurate that they lined up precisely with the sunrise every year on the winter solstice? And that while Europe was in chaos during the Dark Ages, Ireland was the bright light of civilisation, the Harvard or Oxford of its day, churning out manuscripts and artistic marvels by the lorry load? No? Well, shame on you, you ignorant galoot.

Never mind, you can catch up on five thousand years of Irish history in a couple of hours and do it all slap bang in the middle of Dublin. Welcome to The National Museum of Ireland, which holds a great number of Ireland's most renowned treasures.

Actually, The National Museum of Ireland is made up of four museums in four different buildings: Archaeology and Natural History, both in Kildare Street; Decorative Arts in Collins Barracks, just over 2km from O'Connell Street; and The Museum of Country Life in Castlebar, just over 200km from O'Connell Street, which is, admittedly, a bit of a walk. While all of the museums have a great deal going for them, we'll concentrate on the archaeology one because we're too lazy to talk about all the others. The archaeology museum isn't huge by international standards, but then great things often come in small packages, and they've packed a lot in here.

The museum building itself is a treasure. You'll find it in Kildare Street, next door to Leinster House. Purpose-built, it opened in 1890 and its entrance and rotunda were modelled on the Pantheon in Rome. The interior features elaborate ironwork and splendid mosaic floors. But you

probably won't even notice any of that as you'll be too busy looking at the world's finest collection of precious Celtic metalwork, the creepy bog bodies that ended their days with an axe in the brain, and the Iron and Bronze Age displays that show what a clever bunch of gougers we were.

Like most museums, this one has more stuff than you could look at in a month of Sundays (two million artefacts), so while you should dander about at your leisure and have a good gawk at anything that takes your fancy, including any other shapely/hunky tourist you might fancy, we're going to make it easier by pointing out the bits you absolutely should not miss, but not the bits on the tourist you fancy.

♣ Prehistoric Ireland

One of the first exhibitions you'll encounter. Here you can see a re-creation of a Passage Tomb alongside weapons, tools and utensils from the Stone, Bronze and Iron Ages, including the earliest known musical instruments—horns that would have produced a deep, reverberating and irritating blast of noise, not unlike Jedward. What not to miss here—and it's hard to miss—is the fifteen-metre long-boat, hollowed out from a single oak tree. One of the largest of its kind ever found, the boat is over four thousand years old.

♣ Ireland's gold

This is one of the most important collections of Bronze Age gold objects in Europe. It is mostly jewellery and attachments for clothing that were worn on special occasions, like a wedding, a beheading or a disembowelment. There were gansey loads of gold jewellery found in Ireland and nobody really knows where they got all the gold. But when we find the source again, you can expect the entire nation to descend on it in a feeding frenzy. But all that glitters in this room really is gold.

♣ The Treasury

Next stop on this floor, The Treasury, contains some of Ireland's most iconic archaeological pieces, many of which are priceless. Here are the ones not to miss:

♣ The Ardagh Chalice

Small it may be—about the height of a pint glass—but it is the greatest example of Celtic art ever discovered. It was found in 1868 by boys digging for spuds near Ardagh in County Limerick and was probably hidden there in the eighth century while some Vikings were plundering the area and ravishing the local wenches. Fortunately for us, whatever poor eejit hid it probably got an axe in his chest as he never came back to retrieve it. It is elaborately and intricately decorated with gold, gilt bronze, brass, and pewter (see photo on page 74) and is constructed from over three hundred and fifty separate pieces, like a really, really big and expensive Airfix model.

♣ The Tara Brooch

Another priceless masterpiece. Look closely and marvel at the patience of the lads who carved out the tiny, intricate gold and silver interlacing patterns. The brooch has no religious associations and was probably made for some powerful head-the-ball or his mot around 700 AD, its function being to fasten his/her cloak.

♣ The Derrynaflan Chalice

Similar to the Ardagh Chalice, but not quite as elaborate, it was only discovered in 1980 in Tipperary. Yet another masterpiece, this is second only to the Ardagh Chalice and your pint glass in terms of precious drinking vessels. Actually, it was more likely used to hold communion bread. It was the subject of a long drawn-out court case because the discoverers wanted five million pounds to hand it over, which they didn't get, especially as the feckers didn't have permission to search the monastic site where they found it. The case eventually led to a change in the law concerning archaeological discoveries.

The much-journeyed jewellery

Most of the objects in this part of the museum are named after the place they were found. But the Tara Brooch is misnamed, and has an interesting tale behind its discovery. It was actually found in 1850 on a beach in Bettystown, County Meath by an old woman. Or so she claimed. It is more likely the clever oul' bat found it on a farm, but didn't want the farmer to claim it. She sold it to a Dublin jeweller who called it the Tara Brooch, after The Hill of Tara, which was the seat of Ireland's ancient High Kings, also in Meath. You could hardly blame him, as 'The Bettystown Brooch' doesn't have quite the same ring to it. He exhibited it in his Dublin shop for a while, surrounded by replicas, which he was soon selling by the dozen. (A lot of Irish jewellery has been modelled on it ever since.). The brooch was eventually displayed at the Great Exhibition in London and the Exposition Universelle in Paris and then came back to Dublin. Queen Victoria saw it here and ordered it sent to Windsor Castle so she could have a gawk at it and swank about in front of her mirror admiring herself wearing it. But the brooch was at least one thing we managed to stop the 'auld enemy' from nicking, and it was eventually returned to Dublin and ended up in the safe keeping of the National Museum.

♣ The Cross of Cong

The Cross of Cong was designed as a processional cross for the High King of Ireland, Toirdhealbhach Ua Conchobhair, and if you can repeat that when you're rat-arsed later, you'll be given the freedom of Dublin.

The cross features incredibly elaborate gold and silver decoration and originally contained a tiny relic of the True Cross, or at least that's what they believed at the time. The relic has since disappeared, but the cross itself was considered to be of such value that it was hidden for centuries in various places to keep the hands of the invading armies from guess where off it.

♣ The Broighter Gold

Nobody knows exactly why these objects were made, but some think that they were created as an offering to the gods. They were the subject of a long-running court case about a century ago between the British Museum (who had them at the time) and the Royal Irish Academy. We won. Yippee! The torc (a kind of necklace) is one of the finest examples of goldworking from the Iron Age. But the best bit is the miniature boat. Also made of gold, the tiny boat comes complete with eighteen Lilliputian oars, benches and a tiny little rudder. Cute, really cute. Oh, and priceless.

There are lots of other priceless treasures on view here, such as the Shrine of St. Patrick's Bell, The Faddan More Book of Psalms or the Lismore Crozier. So take your time—the dead bodies next door aren't going anywhere.

♣ Kingship & sacrifice: the bog bodies

Moving on to the next exhibit on this floor, you'll encounter a few buckos and cailíns who met a nasty end. Meet the bog bodies. These guys were the unfortunate victims of human sacrifice around 500 BC, their bodies then buried in peat, which has remarkable preservative qualities. What's left of them really look like extras from a Hollywood horror flick. No, take that back, these are genuinely creepy. Also watch out for the 'bog butter', which was preserved in a similar way. Just don't spread any on your toast.

♣ Viking Ireland

Head upstairs and go straight to the Viking exhibition. Ireland was plagued by these bowsies for a few centuries before Brian Boru kicked their arses at the Battle of Clontarf in 1014. But when they'd finally grown tired of defiling our virgins and decided to marry them instead, they contributed significantly to our culture, e.g. many of our names are of Viking origin, such as Doyle, which means 'son of the evil foreigner'. Lots of Irish towns and cities were actually founded originally as Viking settlements, including the one you're standing in. In this exhibition you can see one of the bad guys himself, or what's left of him—his skeleton and his sword. There are loads of other weapons that were used to chop bits off monks, etc. And there's a skull with no less than twenty sword cuts. You can also see a replica of a Viking boat. You can't miss it—it's the big boat-shaped thing.

♣ Medieval Ireland

After the Vikings came the Brits. And so it goes in the museum, as the Medieval Ireland exhibition next door charts the time after the Vikings when our English neighbours decided that they fancied having our country to themselves. Actually it was an Irishman who invited the English here as he wanted

help fighting his enemies in Ireland. But you know how you invite someone to dinner and they won't go home until three in the morning? Well, the English wouldn't go home for seven hundred and fifty years, and only then when Michael Collins and friends showed them the door. This exhibition charts the early centuries of those times, when two cultures and languages existed on the island, and there's loads of interesting stuff to gawk at in the form of weapons, armour, clothes, religious icons and social life.

Other exhibitions on this floor have absolutely nothing to do with Ireland, but are worth a look nonetheless. There's an Egyptian display of things nicked from the ancient sites in the late nineteenth century, mummies and all. And there is also a display called 'Life and Death in the Roman World' with thingies the Romans used in their everyday life and in their everyday afterlife.

THE NATIONAL MUSEUM OF IRELAND (Archaeology),

Kildare Street, Dublin 2

Tel: +353 1 6777444 **Website:** www.museum.ie

Admission is free.

Location: The Museum is just a five-minute walk from

Trinity College, or ten minutes from O'Connell Bridge.

See map.

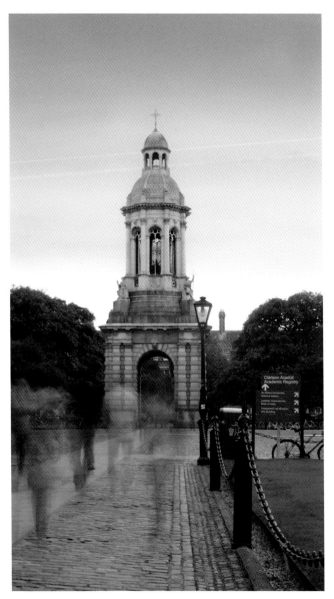

⑩ Trinity College

· ·

Other sights nearby: *Grafton Street, 20m. Temple Bar, 100m. O'Connell Street, 300m. Dublin Castle, 500m.*

There's a popular joke in Trinity College that goes:

| Question: | What does a UCD student (University College Dublin) call a Trinity student after graduation? |
| Answer: | Boss. |

Yes, those deemed worthy to walk the hallowed halls of Ireland's oldest university do like to think of themselves as a cut above, and if you want to see evidence of their superiority, you can visit the students' Pav bar any night and watch them staggering around throwing up on each other in a very posh manner.

♣ The History bit

But never mind all that, because unlike the students, you're here to learn something. And there is a lot of interesting stuff to learn and see in Trinity, like the fact that if you happen to be a Catholic, up until 1970 you would have faced excommunication for attending the university, as it was seen as a bastion of Protestantism. Yes, as recently as four decades ago Ireland was still in the dark ages as regards religion. Luckily all that has changed now, as almost everyone attending Trinity is an atheist.

The Protestant thing all began back in 1592, when Queen Liz I, who referred to Ireland as *'that rude and barbarous nation'*, decided to try and civilise us. So, in between butchering our citizens and chopping people's heads off at court (and she called *us* barbarous?), Liz took time out to grant a royal charter for the establishment of a university.

The college grew and expanded in subsequent centuries to become one of the world's most renowned seats of learning and boasted such famed graduates as Jonathan Swift, Oscar Wilde, Bram Stoker (creator of *Dracula*), renowned philosophers George Berkeley and Edmund Burke, revered Irish national- ists Robert Emmet and Wolfe Tone, Nobel laureates Samuel Beckett (Literature), Ernest Walton (Physics) and Mairead Maguire (Peace), three Presidents of Ireland and one Premier of New Zealand. And of course, Chris de Burgh. But don't let that put you off.

For a couple of hundred years, students wore swords as part of their everyday dress, and reputedly it was even illegal to walk through the grounds without one's sword.

You may only tie the knot in Trinity if you are a graduate or if you are marrying a graduate.

Duels within the grounds were commonplace in the seventeenth and eighteenth centuries.

Apparently there is still an archaic rule in force in Trinity that allows students to request a glass of wine during exams. It is rarely employed however, as most modern students are already pissed when they enter the exam hall.

Walking under the arch from College Green into Parliament Square, the first of the university's many quadrangles, is like stepping from a noisy modern city into an island of eighteenth-century peace—that's if you ignore all the students walking around talking into iPhones and wearing T-shirts that say stuff like 'I Have Too Much Blood In My Alcohol System' or 'Designated Drunk'. Directly ahead you will see the iconic Campanile, which has been towering over the college since 1853. Superstition holds that any student passing under it when the bell tolls will fail their exams. This superstition especially holds true for students who have spent the previous year dossing, missing lectures, getting rat-arsed and smoking pot.

Of course one of the main reasons tourists visit Trinity is to see the Old Library and the Book of Kells. You'll find the library to the right of Library Square, surprise, surprise, which is the green area behind the Campanile. Here's something

BROTHER ENDA WUZ HERE.

to ponder: The library is entitled to a copy of every book published in Ireland or Britain every year, and it now has over five million books. Yes, even those with titles like *Nympho Psycho The Return*. But you won't find that one in the Old Library, which holds the priceless Book of Kells, arguably the most valuable book in the world. It is a stunningly illuminated eighth-century version of the four Gospels. You may be interested to know that the ink was a mixture of soot and apple juice and the parchment was made from the skins of several hundred cows, and, like modern burgers, probably had a few horses thrown in for good measure.

The monks who crafted the Book of Kells also left little reminders of what a pain in the arse work can be, as they scribbled loads of complaints in the margins about their working conditions, etc.: *'I am very cold.' 'New parchment, bad ink; I say nothing more.' 'Oh, my hand!' 'Writing is excessive drudgery. It crooks your back, it dims your sight, it twists your stomach.'* The Book of Kells is undoubtedly Ireland's most viewed book.

A tall tale

In the eighteenth and nineteenth centuries, students of Trinity's Anatomy Department were not above using cadavers stolen by grave-robbers to further their knowledge. But the bounders went one step further in 1760, in the case of Cornelius McGrath, an Irish giant who, at sixteen years old, measured seven feet three inches. (He suffered from acromegaly, which results in excess growth hormone). Cornelius became so famous that he was persuaded to embark on tours all over Europe, where the nobility would pay to come along with their wives and gawk at the unfortunate lump. Finally he returned to Ireland where he struck up a friendship with some Trinity students, who obviously considered the whole thing a 'lark'. Poor Cornelius kicked the bucket, aged twenty-four, and his 'friends' showed their respect by stealing his corpse the day he died and dissecting him. His bones are still on display in Trinity's Anatomy Department.

The Library incorporates The Long Room, which is a stunning 65-metre room with a vaulted ceiling and housing 200,000 old books. It was built in the eighteenth and nineteenth centuries and among its treasures is one of the few surviving copies of the 1916 Proclamation of the Irish Republic, which was read outside the General Post Office in 1916 by Patrick Pearse at the start of the Easter Rising. Trivia: Fans of *Star Wars* might notice that the room bears a striking resemblance to the Jedi Temple in *Star Wars 2: Attack of the Clones*, although

LUKE... I AM... YOUR LECTURER.

the producers maintained that this was just a coincidence. Yeah, right.

The Long Room also contains the Brian Boru Harp (also known as the Trinity College Harp), although in all probability Brian Boru had been dead four hundred years when it was made. Brian, for your information, was the guy who defeated the Vikings in the Battle of Clontarf in 1014, where he met his end. The harp most likely dates from the fifteenth century, and its left-facing image is the national symbol of Ireland, which you'll find on our euros, and more importantly, the right-facing image of the harp is the Guinness logo, with which fact you'll be boring people later in the pub.

Now go out and have a good wander around the place as there's lots more to see, like the fun **Science Gallery**, which features regularly changing and usually fascinating exhibitions; the wonderful and quirky **Douglas Hyde Gallery**, featuring contemporary art; and **The Geological Museum**, where, among other things, you can see Mesozoic ostracods and Upper Palaeozoic miospores—try saying that when you've had six pints.

By the way, Trinity is almost always open to the public, it being a working university, and you can wander around taking snaps if you like. But the best way to appreciate it is to take one of the entertaining tours, which happen every half hour, departing from just inside the main entrance. The tour price includes entry into the Long Room and Book of Kells exhibition.

Having done all of that, you'll probably know more about Trinity College than most of the spotty-faced students. Yes, you've graduated and are now entitled to put the letters P.T.C.B. after your name. Congratulations, you are now a Professor of Trinity College Bullshit.

TRINITY COLLEGE, College Street,Dublin 2
BOOK OF KELLS, **Tel:** +353 (0)1 8962320
Website: www.bookofkells.ie
DOUGLAS HYDE GALLERY, Tel:+ 353 1 896 1116
Website: douglashydegallery.com
Admission is free.
THE SCIENCE GALLERY, The Naughton Institute, Trinity College Pearse Street
Tel: +353 1 896 4091 **Website:** sciencegallery.com
Admission is free.
THE GEOLOGICAL MUSEUM, Department of Geology, Trinity College
Tel: +353 (0) 1 8961477
Location: Trinity College is about as central as you can get. The main entrance is 200m from O'Connell Street Bridge. **See map.**

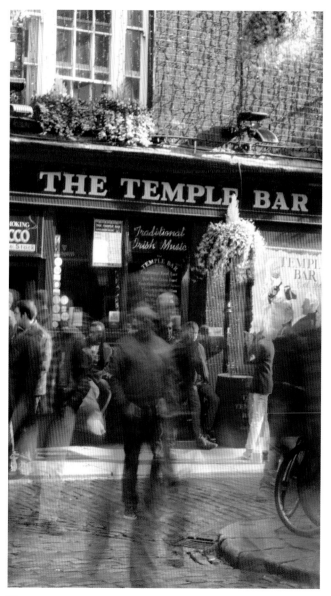

⑪ Temple Bar

. . . .

Other sights nearby: *From Temple Bar Square, Trinity College, 350m. Dublin Castle, 500m. O'Connell Street, 500m. Christ Church Cathedral, 700m.*

There is a wealth of history associated with Temple Bar, which ninety percent of visitors have absolutely no interest in as they just came here to get legless. But, on the off-chance that you are one of the ten percent who would like to know something about the place before you start drinking and seeing double seeing double, well, we're here to serve . . .

♣ The History bit

Most of the historic buildings in Temple Bar date from a couple of hundred years ago, but the pattern of the streets is based on the medieval layout. Unfortunately, none of the actual medieval buildings survive.

The area's boundaries are Dame Street to the south, the River Liffey to the north, **Westmoreland Street** to the east and **Fishamble Street** to the west. The official version is that the place was named after Sir William Temple, a local hob-nob, and that a 'bar' was a riverside walkway. Some historians think that the name was simply borrowed from Temple Bar in London.

Up to the nineteenth century, the place was a bustling area of traders, taverns, homes, workshops and the odd brothel or two, which served to keep a smile on the faces of the traders, tavern keepers, homeowners and workshop workers. As the city expanded, the area slowly declined so that by the late twentieth century the place had become a bit of a kip, with many of its buildings in a tumbledown state. Naturally, we decided that it had to be wiped from the face of the earth so that we could build a big ugly bus depot. Luckily, the then Taoiseach (Prime Minister) Charles Haughey put a stop to the destruction. As it happened, while waiting for the bus depot to be built, many of the buildings had been temporarily rented out for next to nothing, which had attracted lots of artists to the area, they being perennially broke. It also had lots of artisan food and clothes shops, galleries and the like. A couple of tax breaks and a few licks of paint later and, hey presto, Temple Bar had become Dublin's cultural quarter/left bank/pub crawl central.

Temple Bar trivia

Handel's *Messiah* was first performed in Fishamble Street on 13 April 1742 and a performance of the work is held there every year on the same date.

The famous Irish revolutionary group 'The Society of United Irishmen' was formed in a pub in Eustace Street in 1791. The rebellion they led in 1798 was brutally crushed and one of its most famous leaders, Wolfe Tone, sentenced to be hanged. But he cheated the executioner by cutting his own throat. Ugh.

Part of Fownes Street used to be called Bagnio Slip, a bagnio being a term back then for brothel. So they didn't exactly keep these places a secret. It's kind of like having a street nowadays called 'Brothel Avenue' or 'Whorehouse Road'.

Nowadays you'll find many laudable Irish cultural institutions in the narrow, cobbled streets. These include The Gallery of Photography, The **Irish Film Institute**, which shows arty movies where everyone gets killed in the end, The Ark Children's Cultural Centre, the Temple Bar Music Centre, the Arthouse Multimedia Centre, **Temple Bar Gallery and Studio**, The **Project Arts Centre** and the **Gaiety School of Acting**.

You'll also find any number of restaurants, ranging from the expensive to the inexpensive, to the 'cheap as a slapper's make-up' kind. It also has regular markets and interesting little art galleries, clothes and food shops and plenty of kitsch touristy places that sell things like plastic leprechauns baring their arses which is just what you always wanted on your mantelpiece.

There are two small squares in Temple Bar. Meeting House Square is tucked away between Eustace Street and Sycamore Street and can be covered with big, fancy, tent-like things at the touch of a button. It is a venue for cultural events, film screenings and so on, and there's a food market there every Saturday. It is also the location of the free and always interesting Gallery of Photography. The other one is Temple Bar Square, which is slap bang in the middle of the area and a popular meeting place. There are a few coffee shops and ice cream parlours here, so you can sit outside in the rain feeling colder than the chocolate ice cream you're eating. Just off Temple Bar Square you'll see a narrow lane that leads to Merchant's Arch, which is part of one of the oldest and nicest buildings. It was originally built for merchant tailors and the arch provides a convenient short-cut to the Ha'penny Bridge, which has become something of an icon of Dublin.

The bridge is a couple of hundred years old and because it put the ferries out of business when it was built, the ferry operators were allowed to charge a toll for crossing, hence the name.

And if you haven't cottoned on to this by now, Temple Bar also boasts a pub or two, or three. (*See* Dublin Pubs for our favourites.) Among the more well-known places to get fluthered are The Temple Bar (geddit?), The Oliver St. John Gogarty (named after a famous Irish poet, author, politician and, wait-for-it, otolaryngologist—look it up), The Porterhouse, Fitzsimons and The Auld Dubliner, not to mention a rake of others.

It you want to see Temple Bar at its best, visit during daytime, when the streets are relatively quiet and you might actually get a seat in a pub. After dark, parts of the area may become paganistic and you may witness some of the rituals associated with this, such as gangs of girls with skirts that could pass as belts, wearing their knickers on their heads and reeling from side to side, singing, 'I'm getting married in the morning' and 'My ding-a-ling' at the same time. You may also spot the occasional drunken male. You can often identify these from the fact that they are face down in the gutter still clutching a half-finished pint of stout in one hand and a punctured inflatable woman in the other. Having said that, not every night-time visitor to the area is on a stag/hen night and you can still find relatively quiet streets with nice pubs and restaurants.

All things considered, Temple Bar is deadly. (Don't worry—check the Dublin Slang Guide!)

TEMPLE BAR, Dublin 2
Website: www.templebar.ie
GALLERY OF PHOTOGRAPHY, Meeting House Square, Temple Bar
Tel: +353 1 671 4654
Admission is free.
IRISH FILM INSTITUTE, 6 Eustace Street, Temple Bar.
Bookings: 01 679 3477 **Website:** www.ifibooking.ie
Location: Temple Bar is right in the middle of Dublin, on the banks of the River Liffey, and a short walk from O'Connell Bridge or Trinity College. **See map.**

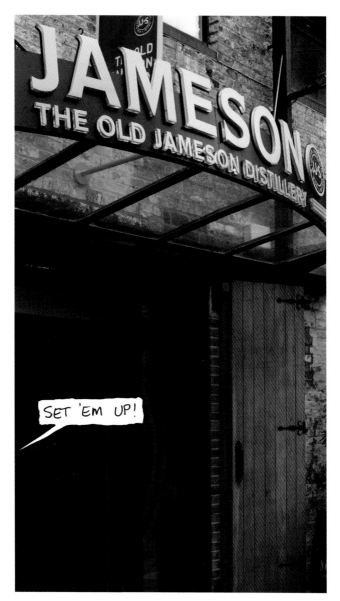

⑫ Old Jameson Distillery

● ●

Other sights nearby: *Christ Church Cathedral, 800m. Guinness Storehouse, 1km. O'Connell Street/GPO, 1.2km.*

Just in case you haven't had enough alcohol advertising at the Guinness Storehouse, and would prefer something a tad stronger than 'the black stuff', i.e., 'a drop of the hard stuff', then, not too far away, as you head back into the city along the northside Liffey quays, on Bow Street, you'll find the Old Jameson Distillery. Except it's not actually a distillery any more, as that moved to Cork in the 1970s, but this is the location of the original, and some alcohol-lovers prefer the 'intimacy' of this tour to the Guinness extravaganza.

You'll get to see all of the old equipment being operated by real live mannequins, who move with the same speed as a Dublin County Council road worker. There are also lots of dioramas and interesting historical bits and you'll get to hear all about the process of making Jameson, from storing the grain, to making the barrels, to how they achieve the perfection of the finished product.

Jameson is Triple Distilled, as your guide will explain, making it the smoothest and finest-tasting whiskey in the world. And here's a bit of knowledge to impress your friends with later in the evening as you raise your glass: Irish whiskey is always spelled with an 'e'; if it says 'whisky' on the bottle, it's not Irish!

Now, normally, whenever you are asked to volunteer, our advice would be DON'T—anyone who's ever ended up on stage being hypnotised will agree. But, in this case, when the tour guide asks for volunteers, PUT YOUR HANDS UP. On each tour, eight people are chosen at random to do what they call a 'Tutored Whiskey Tasting', in other words, you get to compare Irish whiskey with leading Scotch and American brands. And then you are given a certificate saying that you are a 'Qualified Irish Whiskey Taster'. Something for you to frame and cherish forever!

Of course you are free to declare that you prefer Scotch or American after the tasting, at which point the guide will push a button opening a trapdoor beneath your feet, dropping you deep into the heart of Dublin's sewerage system, which was built in the mid-nineteenth century, which fact you may as well ponder as you plummet to a horrible end.

And the good news is that even if you aren't one of the chosen tasters, everybody gets a free glass of Jameson, either straight or as a cocktail, at the end of the tour.

By the way, if you do become addicted to the stuff when you get home, the humongous chandelier in the distillery made from Jameson bottles might give you an idea of what to do with the empties.

OLD JAMESON DISTILLERY, Bow Street, Smithfield Village, Dublin 7
Tel: +353 (1) 8072355 **Website:** www.tours.jamesonwhiskey.com
Location: The Distillery is approx 1.3km from O'Connell Street. It is beside a LUAS stop. Turn left on Bow Street and go straight ahead. **See map.**

⑬ O'Connell Street & The GPO

• •

Other sights nearby: *From GPO, Garden of Remembrance, 500m. Trinity College, 600m.*

In its time poor O'Connell Street has been widened, narrowed, demolished, rebuilt, bombarded, rebuilt, bombarded again and rebuilt again. It has had three names and has witnessed periods of splendour, tackiness, beauty, tragedy and glory. So, if nothing else, it's interesting.

There's a common claim made that it is the widest main thoroughfare in Europe, but really, has anyone gone out with a measuring tape and compared the various main streets in Europe? And at the end of the day, as Dubliners would say, who gives a flying feck? (Although they might say it in stronger language. But if you're interested in that sort of thing, then let us tell you that O'Connell Street is 49 metres wide at its southern end and 46 metres at its northern end and is 503 metres long. You really needed to know that, didn't you?

The History bit

The street was originally laid out as Drogheda Street in the seventeenth century and then widened to its record-breaking (ironic) width in the mid-eighteenth century, when it was re-named Sackville Street after some lord who nobody in Ireland had ever heard of. At that point it only extended to within about one hundred metres of the River Liffey. But in the late eighteenth century the street was extended to the river and, with the opening of the Carlisle Bridge (now O'Connell Bridge), the street's fortunes took off and business boomed—and it was regarded as one of the finest thoroughfares in the world.

The nineteenth century saw the building of many iconic structures such as The Palatial Mart (now the site of Clery's Department Store), the towering Nelson's Pillar, fine hotels like the Gresham and the Metropole and of course the GPO, or General Post Office. So there we were, with one of the most admired streets on the planet, so what did we do? Well, naturally, we obliterated it! Well, us and our British friends, that is. But O'Connell Street really gets to write itself into the history books in the early part of the twentieth century . . .

The GPO and the Easter Rising

Imagine the scene. There you are on a nice spring morning in April 1916, walking into the GPO to buy a stamp so you can send your sweetheart a smoochy love letter. Next thing there are hordes of guys sticking guns in your face and proclaiming a free, independent Ireland.

main columns, which are still visible. A statue in the main foyer depicting the death of the Irish mythological hero Cú Chulainn (pr: *Ku-Kullen*) commemorates the Rising. A small museum in the GPO has, among other stuff, an original copy of the Proclamation and also gives an insight into the poor Post Office staff who were caught up in the Rising and really wished they'd pulled a sickie that Easter Monday.

Monto

The Monto was an area to the east of O'Connell Street famed during the nineteenth century and early twentieth century as the biggest red light district in Europe, if not the world. It took its name from Montgomery Street (now Foley Street) and at its orgasmic pinnacle it had over 1,600 prostitutes providing horizontal refreshment mostly to lonely British Army soldiers. Ironically, it was also like a rabbit warren of IRA activity during the War of Independence, with many of the patriotic hookers providing safe houses for the rebels. The Monto was frequented by many notables, including the then Prince of Wales (later King Edward VII), who is reputed to have lost his virginity there. His excuse was most likely that he wanted to let his subjects have a closer look at his royal sceptre. The Monto found literary fame when it featured in James Joyce's masterpiece *Ulysses*—two of the central characters, Leopold Bloom and Stephen Dedalus, pay a visit to a brothel there. It is also the subject of a popular folk song, 'Take her up to Monto', by the Dubliners.

YER WAN'S DOING HER 'BIT' FOR HER COUNTRY.

♣ Attack of the property speculators

In the years after the Rising, the War of Independence and the Civil War, O'Connell Street was rebuilt and regained much of its former glory. But if Dubs thought the British guns had done a lot of damage, they hadn't seen what city councillors and property speculators were capable of. For several decades up to the nineties, they had a free-for-all, demolishing fine buildings so they could provide us with much-needed burger joints and tacky amusement arcades.

Thankfully, the street has undergone a renaissance in recent years, with much of the tat removed, the paths widened, traffic reduced, new street furnishings and sculpture and the protection of what's left of the street's architectural heritage.

♣ Monuments to our past

You might be wondering where O'Connell Street gets its name. No? Well, you're going to find out anyway. If you're standing in the middle of O'Connell Bridge, and haven't been hit by a truck yet, then looking straight ahead you will see a fine statue of Daniel O'Connell, The Liberator. It's a bit of a misnomer actually, as he didn't completely liberate us, but did win the Catholic population of Ireland emancipation back in 1829, and, unlike the guys in 1916, he did it by purely pacifist means. Four winged victories surround Dan, representing his virtues: Patriotism, Courage, Eloquence and Fidelity. Poor Courage has had a rough time of it—you can still see a bullet hole from the Rising in her right boob, and then, in 1969, northern loyalists tried to blow up the statue and only succeeded in sending Courage winging her way temporarily to heaven before she was restored.

Another statue to look out for is the wonderfully expressive monument to Jim Larkin, the early twentieth-century Trade Union leader, which stands in the central median, almost directly opposite the GPO, and which carries the inscription 'The great appear great because we are on our knees: Let us rise.'

Nelson's Pillar

The site where the Spire of Dublin now stands was originally occupied by a 134-foot stone column crowned with a statue of Admiral Nelson, which stood there for one hundred and fifty years. Even before independence, there was much debate about having a relic of the British Empire displayed so prominently in Dublin's main street. Eventually, having some English hero lording it over them became too much to bear and in 1955, a group of students tried to melt the statue with flamethrowers! Had they been students of geology, they might have known that Portland stone wouldn't melt. Where they failed, however, the IRA succeeded, and in 1966, fifty years after the Rising, they managed to blow up the structure in the middle of the night without injuring a single Dubliner, one of the few humane achievements of the modern IRA. The remains of the column had then to be blown up by the army, during which attempt they broke almost every window in O'Connell Street.

Heading north, there's a statue in the central median beyond the GPO, which you might be interested in, especially if your itinerary includes getting rat-arsed in several hundred pubs. It is that of Father Theobald Mathew, the man who essentially saved Ireland from drowning in a sea of booze in the early nineteenth century. It was said that he had originally been a heavy drinker but one night saw a vision of a very strange bird, who told him to change his ways, an experience anyone who's been really fluthered will have shared. After that he began convincing people to pledge never to drink again. And, believe it or not, he managed to enroll three million people—half of Ireland's population at the time—into the Pioneer Total Abstinence Society. He had similar success in northern England and even convinced six hundred thousand Yanks to climb on the wagon for life. He was not a popular man with the breweries . . .

At the far north end of the street stands the impressive obelisk and statue to Charles Stewart Parnell, another legendary Irish nationalist leader of the late nineteenth century and the man most responsible for getting all our land back from British landlords, which they'd simply nicked over the previous centuries.

♣ Shops and other stuff

The landmark shop on O'Connell Street is Clery's Department Store, almost directly opposite the GPO. The business began in 1853 and the original building was flattened during the Rising. The present fine building dates from the twenties and used to feature its own ballroom; the interior still has a nifty staircase. Clery's clock is a well-known meeting point for Dubs, particularly for a romantic rendezvous, and hopefully a quick snog.

If you fancy a movie, the Savoy Cinema is Ireland's oldest, dating from 1929, and originally had an amazing capacity of almost three thousand. The cinema now has six screens and is the venue of choice for most big event film premieres.

The Spire of Dublin, which stands almost opposite the GPO, was erected in 2003 and, at 121 metres, is the tallest sculpture in the world. The tip of it lights up at night as a kind of beacon, so that drunk people can find their bearings from almost anywhere in the city. Opinion on it among Dubs varies between 'It's grand' to 'It's a wojus-lookin' yoke.' (*See* also panel 'Statue nicknames', page 46)

♣ Henry Street/Moore Street

If you're facing the GPO, the street on the right leading off O'Connell Street is Henry Street, the most popular shopping

street in Dublin. It is considered to be a kind of downmarket version of Grafton Street, but usually only by snobby eejits. It is an interesting street to do a bit of shopping, and it will probably cost you a few bob less. It is completely pedestrianised and there are over two hundred shops on Henry Street, including Arnotts, the oldest and largest department store in Dublin, which opened its doors in 1843. Besides that, there are the usual mix of international chain stores and a few smaller independent shops selling everything from bananas to inverted toenail clippers. There are also a couple of shopping centres; the Ilac and the Jervis Shopping Centre, which is the biggest in the city centre.

At the other end of the scale you'll see a good few stalls selling T-shirts, jewellery and wind-up boobs that walk and sing, and that sort of thing. About a hundred metres along on the right you'll find Moore Street, famed as the place where the rebels finally surrendered in 1916, and also an iconic Dublin fruit and veg market. It is usually very busy and colourful, with lots of stalls overflowing with apples, peaches and sticks of celery, in case you're in a healthy diet frame of mind. Much of the street's colour comes from the sellers themselves, who are usually working-class ladies with thick Dublin accents shouting things like 'Gedyerorngesforforayouro' ('Get your oranges four for a euro'). Usually great value to be had here, and the produce is first class.

♣ Street smart

O'Connell Street can be a great place to visit, especially by day, when you will have an eclectic mix of culture, history, shopping, dining and entertainment to choose from. After dark, and particularly late at night, it may become a bit rough, with all sorts of drunken eejits and drug-addled gougers staggering around. The minimal police presence on the street is a regular topic of complaint on the Irish airwaves, and there's always some politician ready with an excuse that makes absolutely no sense whatsoever. The smart thing to do, obviously, is avoid it at night, but by all means don't miss it during daylight hours.

O'CONNELL STREET, Dublin 1
GENERAL POST OFFICE, O'Connell Street, Dublin 1
Admission is free.
AN POST MUSEUM, in General Post Office, **Tel:**+353 1 705 7000
Admission charged.
Location: O'Connell Street is slap bang in the middle of Dublin.
See map.

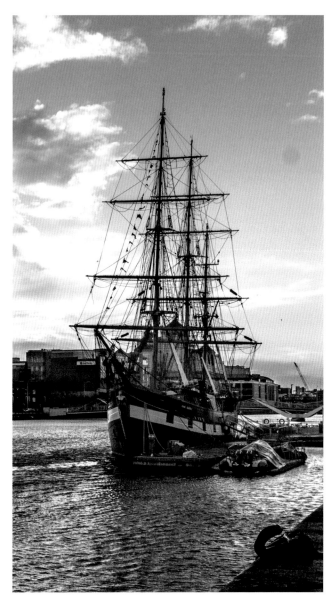

⑭ Jeanie Johnston Tall Ship and Famine Museum

• •

Other sights nearby: *Windmill Lane Studios, 500m. O'Connell Street/GPO, 1km.*

The high seas beckon, you landlubbers. Shiver me timbers, anchors aweigh and let's get three sheets to the wind for we're bound for Amereecay. Well, not so much the high seas as the River Liffey. And you won't be going to Amereecay or anywhere else for that matter, although later tonight you might well be three sheets to the wind.

Enough of this seafaring guff. The *Jeanie Johnston* Tall Ship and Famine Museum will let you pass an enjoyable and educational hour or so. The ship—and it is a real ship— is docked at Custom House Quay, close to the city centre and a long way from the high seas. It is a replica of an actual ship that sailed between County Kerry and Canada during the Great Famine, bringing very skinny people across to the new world. Reconstructed over a ten-year period, the ship cost three times its original estimate to build. In fact it would probably have been cheaper to build a bridge to Quebec. But as a result, the museum bit and authentic re-creations are put together very nicely, not unlike Jennifer Lopez.

♣ The History bit

In case you've been living off-planet your entire life, you will probably have heard that we had a bit of a food shortage here back in the mid-nineteenth century. Well, actually, the country was stuffed with food, but the wealthy landlords who owned it all were exporting it so they could become even wealthier. Their tenant farmers survived almost exclusively on one crop—the good old spud—and when it was attacked by blight for five successive years, people starved. Conservative estimates put the number of dead at a million. Double that number fled the country on famine ships, like the *Jeanie Johnston*, bound for a new life in America, South America, Canada, Britain, Australia and loads of other places. Which is why every Hollywood movie credit list is crammed with names like Seamus Murphy, Mick Kelly, Brigid O'Reilly, Paddy Kennedy, Nora O'Dea, etc. But their ancestors were the lucky ones because usually you had about a one in three chance of kicking the bucket and getting fecked overboard. Remarkably, the original *Jeanie Johnston* never lost one passenger in the seven years she sailed. And here's the thing, nowadays the ship, which is a fully seaworthy vessel, is licensed to carry forty people, but back in the 1840s she was regularly carrying about two hundred and fifty. Well, as previously mentioned, they were all very thin.

Deadly Irish Roots

Tragic as it was, one of the direct consequences of the emigration that accompanied the Great Famine is that there are now loads of famous people around the world whose ancestors all set sail from Ireland in ships like the *Jeanie Johnston*. Among those you can number industrialist Henry Ford, revolutionary Che Guevara, actors Mel Gibson and George Clooney, U.S. comedian Conan O'Brien, rock star Bruce Springsteen and boxer Muhammad Ali. And there are gazillions more.

Of course, the most famous of all of these was John F. Kennedy, the thirty-fifth President of the United States of America. What is not so widely known is that the man who assassinated him, Lee Harvey Oswald, was also a direct descendant of a famine emigrant—his great-grandmother was one Mary Tonry of County Sligo. Sorry about that, America . . .

♣ All aboard

Below decks you'll be met by several smelly and really hungry-looking Irish peasants. Don't worry, they're all dummies. But they will give you a sense of what it was like to spend seven weeks in one of these ships—the cramped little bunk spaces, the bad food, the lack of hygiene, the stench (sounds like

a cheap package holiday in Benidorm). But you also get to learn what became of some of the actual passengers who sailed in the original *Jeanie Johnston*, which adds a whole layer of interest to proceedings.

There are lots of fascinating things to see and hear. Bunk space, for example, was at a premium—four adults to six foot square—so you could expect to wake up in the middle of the night with some else's arse, or worse, in your face. And you'll hear stories like that of Nicholas Johnston Reilly who joined the maiden voyage in the mid-Atlantic: he was born on board, survived, and was named after the ship. And keeping up the astonishing record of having never lost a passenger or crew member, even when the *Jeanie Johnston* eventually sank on a return voyage, the crew managed to climb into the rigging and wait there until rescued.

Above decks you'll also get to hear about the vessel's painstaking construction as a fully ocean-worthy replica of a nineteenth-century tall ship. She's actually taken part in the Tall Ships' Race. Ok, she only came sixtieth out of sixty-five, but still. And keep an eye out for the ship's figurehead who's quite heavy on the upper deck herself. In fact, she rivals the Molly Malone statue as the bustiest in Ireland, and she's in full colour.

♣ Famine Memorial

While you're in the neighbourhood and on a related topic, watch out for the moving Famine Memorial just along the quay (that's *moving*, as in 'tugging the heart strings'—they don't actually move). By sculptor Rowan Gillespie, it depicts a number of life-size famine victims walking towards the coffin ships which would have been berthed on the Dublin quayside.

Rock the boat

If you've visiting the *Jeanie Johnston*, and if you're a rock music fan, you might fancy a short trip across the river to make a commonly taken pilgrimage to **Windmill Lane Studios** where it all began for a little Irish band you might have heard of, called U2. Bring your camera to snap some of the graffiti that has been layered on over the decades. Scientists in the future will no doubt use advanced scanning techniques to reveal sprayed-over, mysterious texts such as *'I luv ye Bono, yer bleedin' grate! Jennifer 2/5/90 xxxxxxxx'* or *'I've found what I'm looking for, it's you Adam xxxx Grazyna April 88'*. We cannot recommend that you contribute to the graffiti wall, as it is officially illegal, and occasionally temporary signs are posted warning tourists of this. But usually the signs themselves are obliterated by graffiti. Whether you want to write your own name in rock history is entirely up to you . . . Windmill Lane Studios opened in 1978 (it was originally a warehouse). In its early days it was used to record Irish traditional music, but all that changed when U2 decided to use the studio in the eighties. They would go on to record legendary albums there like 'War' and 'The Joshua Tree'. The list of rock stars who subsequently recorded there is impressive: R.E.M, The Rolling Stones, Sinead O'Connor, Van Morrison, Elvis Costello and gansey loads of others. The Spice Girls also used the studio, but hey, let's not hold that against it. The studio is just across the Sean O'Casey foot-bridge, almost directly opposite the ship. See map if you still haven't found what you're looking for.

JEANIE JOHNSTON TALL SHIP AND FAMINE MUSEUM,
Custom House Quay, I.F.S.C. Dublin 1
Tel: +353 (0)1 4730111 **Website:** www.jeaniejohnston.ie
Admission charged.
Location: The ship is 1km from O'Connell Street.
See map.

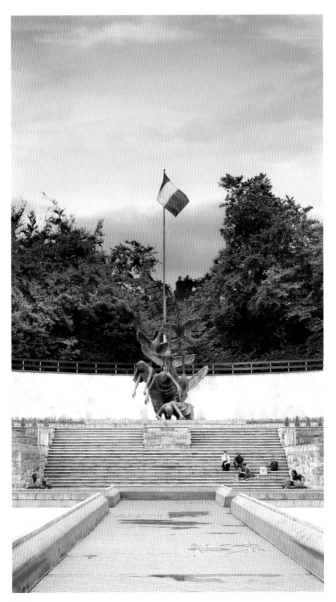

⑮ The Garden of Remembrance & Parnell Square

• •

Other sights nearby: *O'Connell Street/GPO, 500m.*

What better place to add to the memory of your trip to Dublin than the Garden of Remembrance? After all, with the number of pubs you're planning to visit, you'll probably remember very little else.

The Garden of Remembrance is a little oasis in the heart of the city, a pleasant place to escape the noise of the traffic and the souvenir shops in O'Connell Street selling Father Ted T-shirts, leprechaun hats and chocolates in the shape of shamrocks and boobs. You'll find it at the northern end of Parnell Square, which is just at the top of O'Connell Street. This is a lovely place to bring your take-out coffee and Danish pastry and relax in the peaceful, floral surroundings while you muse upon the heroism of Ireland's freedom fighters and contemplate the meaning of life, etc.

♣ The History bit

The Garden was opened in 1966 during the fiftieth anniversary of the Easter Rising, although it commemorates all those who died in the cause of Irish freedom in various uprisings including:

The 1798 Rebellion (We lost that one)
The 1803 Rebellion (We lost that one)
The 1848 Rebellion (We lost that one)
The 1867 Rebellion (We lost that one)

The 1916 Easter Rising (We lost that one)

The 1919–21 War of Independence (Yeehaa, we kicked arse!)

Whatever else, you certainly can't call us quitters. It is located close to the site where the Irish Volunteers were founded in 1913 and where the prisoners were held overnight after the 1916 Rising. And it was actually opened by

one of those prisoners, Éamon de Valera (affectionately known as 'Dev') who was the then President of Ireland. In case you're wondering, de Valera obviously isn't a very Irish name—his Ma was Irish and his Da was Cuban. Dev himself was actually born in America, a fact which probably saved him from being stuck up against a wall and shot in 1916.

♣ What's there?

The garden was designed by Dáithí Hanly, which *is* a very Irish name. It takes the form of a sunken pool in the shape of a cross, at the head of which is a raised platform holding an impressive sculpture of the Children of Lir by Oisín Kelly, which is another very Irish name. Who were the Children of Lir, you may ask, or you may not, for that matter. Well, you're going to find out one way or the other. They were mythological children who were magically turned into swans and lived on a lough for nine hundred years until the spell was broken and they were turned back into humans again. So the sculpture symbolises the rebirth of Ireland after nine hundred years of pesky English oppression. It was actually more like 754 years,

8 months and 15 days, but who's counting? The other thing is that when the children were turned back into humans they sort of dropped dead almost immediately, as they were now nine centuries old. So the symbolism only works so far, as, luckily, everyone in Ireland didn't drop dead the moment we'd won back our freedom.

You'll notice a mosaic depicting broken weapons on the bottom of the pool. In ancient Celtic Ireland when two enemy tribes had finished hacking the bejaysus out of each other and agreed on a truce, they smashed their weapons and threw them into the nearest river. So the mosaic is representative of the ending of hostilities between Ireland and Britain, just in case you couldn't work that out for yourself.

♣ Your Majesty

In April 2011, Britain's Queen Elizabeth II made a trip to Ireland, which was the first time a British monarch had been here in precisely one hundred years. The purpose of the visit was to officially bury the hatchet, and for once, not in each other's heads. The most symbolic moment of the trip came when she visited the Garden of Remembrance and, before the watching world, respectfully bowed her head before a wreath laid in honour of those who had died in the 1916 Rising.

♣ Square and Fair

While you're in the vicinity, **Parnell Square** itself is worth a wander. One of Dublin's original Georgian squares, it has lots more besides its architecture. It is named after legendary Irish statesman, Charles Stewart Parnell. (*See* Glasnevin Cemetery & Museum, page 163.) Walking from the Garden's main entrance back to O'Connell Street, over on the left at No. 25 is where the plans were first made to stage the 1916 Rising, and on the right you'll see the world-renowned Gate Theatre, where the likes of Orson Wells, James Mason and Michael Gambon first strutted their stuff before mega stardom stole them away. Next door, on the corner, is the Ambassador, now a music venue. This was the first place in Ireland to show 'moving pictures' and subsequently became a cinema that could seat over twelve hundred people.

Continuing around past the Ambassador is the fine building that is the Rotunda Hospital, a maternity hospital built in 1745. Gazillions of us Paddies had our first glimpse of the world as we emerged through its doors, having first emerged from our Mammies. Continue all the way around the square back to the rear of the Garden of Remembrance. On the north side of the square is the Hugh Lane Gallery, which was the first public gallery of modern art in the world. It also houses work by Renoir, Manet and Pissaro, in case you fancy musing over some masterpieces. Beyond that, also on the left, is the Dublin Writer's Museum, just next to the church. The museum is a magnificent Georgian mansion, which displays extremely rare first editions of some of Dublin's many literary giants such as *Dracula* by Bram Stoker, Wilde's *The Importance of Being Earnest*, *Ulysses* by Joyce, etc. It also has lots of bits and bobs that once belonged to the great men, such as their typewriters, pens, telephones and even a teddy bear. Appropriately for a book dishing out advice, let us conclude with the words of one of Dublin's greatest writers, Oscar Wilde: 'I always pass on good advice. It is the only thing to do with it. It is never of any use to oneself.'

GARDEN OF REMEMBRANCE, Parnell Square East, Dublin 1
Admission is free.
HUGH LANE GALLERY, Charlemont House, Parnell Square North
Dublin 1
Tel: +353 1 222 5550
Website: www.hughlane.ie
Admission is free.
DUBLIN WRITERS MUSEUM, 18 Parnell Square, Dublin 1
Tel: +353 1 872 2077 **Website:** www.writersmuseum.com
Admission charged.
Location: 5 minutes' walk from O'Connell Street.
See map.

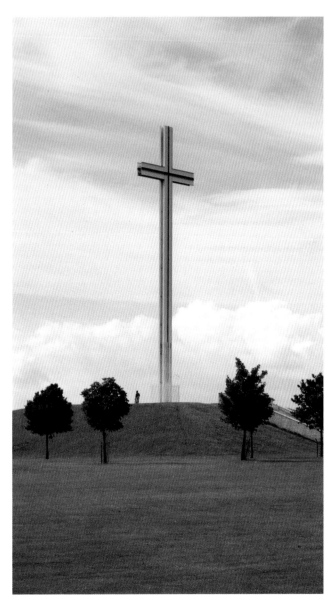

Stuff that's just a little further out (but worth the effort)

⑯ The Phoenix Park

• •

Other sights nearby: *From Parkgate Street entrance, National War Memorial Gardens, nearest entrance 1.2km. Kilmainham Gaol, 1.5km.*

Time for some fresh air. The great outdoors beckons, as right here in Dublin you can experience the wide open landscape of the countryside. Well, sort of. The Phoenix Park is the largest walled park in Europe. And as city parks go, it's feckin' ginormous. It is larger than all of London's parks put together, and Central Park in New York is only a village green in comparison. The exterior wall alone is 11km long. And within it you'll find 1,750 acres of beautiful grassland and tall, broad-leaved trees, not to mention Dublin Zoo, the residences of the President and the U.S. Ambassador, a seventeenth-century castle, an Edwardian mansion, monuments, a fort, flower gardens, lakes, a large herd of deer and lots of people jogging/cycling around trying to reduce the size of their arse. There are 22km of roads, 14km of cycle lanes and 30km of footpaths, and lots and lots of space. The park's name has little connection with the mythical bird of Greek mythology, although there is a phoenix perched atop the monument at the park's centre. There used to be a spring on the land, which produced clear water, or, in Irish, 'fionn uisce'. And if you say that after a night out on the lash it vaguely sounds like 'phoenix', and so the name stuck.

If you like taking a nice long walk, then the Phoenix Park is for you—and there is much to see. If you're a lazy slob, you can even glimpse lots of the sights from a tour bus, many of which visit the park. It is also a very safe place and even has its own sort of police squad of Park Rangers, who have the power to arrest offenders. Those of a romantic nature, or to be more specific, those of a randy nature, should note that there is a by-law that states: 'No person shall act contrary to public morality in the Park'. So if you're planning any hanky panky in the grass, be warned. Mind you, some of the wide open spaces are so large and the grass so wild, that you could probably hold a swingers party there and get away with it. One word of advice: safe as it is during the day, it is not a place you should visit after dark unless you're driving.

The Phoenix Park is just 2½km from O'Connell Street and is very easy to get to. As mentioned, many of the tour buses visit there, but if you want the do-it-yourself version, a short public bus ride will take you to the Parkgate Street main entrance. The LUAS tramline will also take you to within spit-

ting distance of the main gate. But the best way to see as much as possible in the park is probably by bike, and there is a bike hire facility just inside the main entrance at Parkgate Street—more details below.

♣ The History bit

We can thank one particular English chap for the Phoenix Park. Way back in 1662, the Duke of Ormonde established a Royal Hunting Park on the land in case King Charles II ever got bored with bedding his seven mistresses. The land contained pheasants and wild deer, but they quickly realised that when they pursued them with guns and knives, the damn inconsiderate blighters kept flying/running away, so they had to build a huge wall around the area.

It wasn't until 1745 that the Lord Lieutenant of Ireland, Lord Chesterfield, allowed the great unwashed to set foot inside the place. He was actually quite an impressive character—during his short, year-long reign he managed to get rid of a lot of political and civil service jobbery (if only we had his like today), built schools and encouraged industry. And he made a very nice gift to the people by allowing their dirty, commoner feet to stroll about the royal lands of this vast estate. The main avenue in the park, which, incidentally, is over 4km long, is named after him.

We'll catch up on a few more snippets of interesting history as we take a long lazy stroll through the park. So let's get moving.

♣ A walk in the park

Entering from the main gate at Parkgate Street on the eastern end of the park, the first thing to look out for on your right is The Victorian People's Flower Gardens, which name might give you a hint to what's inside. It's sort of a park within a park, and is a reasonable size itself—22 acres—and was opened in 1864 to show off Victorian horticulture at its finest. It has lots of pretty flowerbeds, an ornamental pond, nice walkways and so on, and it's a nice place to go for a picnic with your other half on a warm summer's day. And the chances of you getting one of those in Dublin are roughly the same as the chance you'll be hit by a meteor. The gardens also feature a statue of one of the leaders of the 1916 Rising, Sean Heuston, who was executed in Kilmainham. And, interestingly, there's a plinth nearby which originally had a statue of George William Howard, a former Lord Lieutenant, but which was blown to kingdom come in 1956 by militant republicans who didn't like the idea of some old Lord lording it over them while they ate their picnics.

Murder most foul

The park was the scene of one of the most infamous political murders in Ireland's history, which became known as the 'Phoenix Park Murders'. In 1882, the new Chief Secretary for Ireland, Lord Frederick Cavendish, had just arrived in Ireland, literally a few hours beforehand, and he was strolling home to the Viceregal Lodge (now Áras an Uachtaráin). The Under Secretary for Ireland, Thomas Henry Burke, happened along in a cab and decided to accompany Cavendish on his evening stroll. Boy, was that a mistake. As they neared the Phoenix Monument, seven men surrounded the poor feckers and proceeded to stab them with surgical knives. The pair were dead in seconds—a cross is set into the grass on the spot where they fell.

The assassins were a fanatical nationalist breakaway group who had ironically named themselves 'The Irish National Invincibiles', ironic as within a couple of months most of them had been strung up in nearby Kilmainham Gaol. Their action also had the result of effectively ending the prospect of Home Rule from Britain, which Charles Stewart Parnell had been on the brink of securing. Thanks a bunch, lads.

And talking of old British guys, back on the main avenue directly across from the gardens, you'll see a towering obelisk—the largest one in Europe at 62 metres. That's the Wellington Monument, which was started in 1817 to honour Arthur Wellesley, the Duke of Wellington, he of the welly boot and the Battle of Waterloo, etc. Most people assume he was English, but no, he was a Paddy, not that we're proud to remember him as such, as he was a member of the

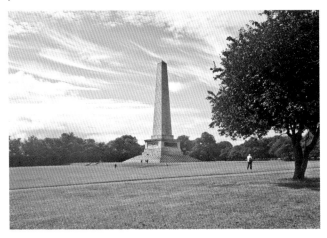

British Ascendancy class, and didn't give a toss about his Irish heritage. In fact, when a colleague remarked on his place of birth, he reputedly replied: 'Being born in a stable does not make one a horse.' So, as you can imagine, old Welly isn't recalled too fondly in Ireland.

Anyway, his obelisk would have been even taller but they ran out of money when building it. Eventually the thing was completed in 1861 but didn't feature the planned statue of him on the top, which is probably just as well as it most likely would have gone the way of Nelson's Pillar. The four large bronze plaques on its sides honour his career and were cast from the metal of enemy cannons from the Battle of Waterloo. There's a metal spike on the top and occasionally during storms the rod attracts lightning, quite spectacularly illuminating the obelisk at night. So at least the thing's good for something.

Back on the main avenue and just beyond the People's Gardens lies Dublin Zoo, one of the finest and oldest zoos in the world. Opened in 1831, it covers an impressive 69 acres and is filled with all manner of wild animals. Just how wild they are

is reflected in the fact that the zoo ran out of food during the 1916 Rising so they solved the problem by killing a load of the animals and feeding them to the rest. Among the strange beasts you can see here are the yellow-backed chattering lory and the scimitar-horned oryx. You really wanted to know that, didn't ye? In 1919 a lion named Slats was born in the zoo and was to achieve stardom as the original lion that growled at you from the middle of the MGM logo.

Back across the avenue and following what is known as the Military Road beyond the Wellington Monument, you will eventually see a big yoke up on top of a small hill on your right. This is called the Magazine Fort. You can get a decent view across the city from up here, but unfortunately the fort itself is closed up. It was built in 1735 to store gunpowder for the British Army. At the time Jonathan Swift immortalised the building in a short satirical verse in which he has a pop at the Irish politicians of the day:

Now here's a proof of Irish sense,
Here Irish wit is seen,
When nothing's left that's worth defence,
We build a Magazine.

During the Rising the rebels actually succeeded in taking over the fort and stealing some weapons, but their plan to blow up the remainder failed when the fuses on the explosives burnt out before they reached the ammo. The eejits really blew it. Or didn't, as it happened.

Bombs away

As mentioned in Chapter 13, dealing with the GPO, the British army almost blew up the Viceregal Lodge in 1916 when the shells aimed at the GPO landed in the grounds, missing their target by a mere three kilometres. But if you think that's lousy shooting, jump forward to WW2, when the Luftwaffe managed to drop a bomb near 'The Dog Pond', shattering windows in the Lodge and the U.S. Ambassador's residence. The German pilot apparently thought he was over Coventry, missing his target by about five hundred kilometres.

Continuing back along Chesterfield Avenue, the trees part to reveal a nice vista opening onto Áras an Uachtaráin (Pr: *or-us un u-uch-ter-awn)*, which literally means 'House of the President' and which used to be the Viceregal Lodge before we won independence and took over all the nice buildings the English folk used to live in. Áras an Uachtaráin is open on Saturdays only. Free admission tickets are issued at the Phoenix Park Visitor Centre, which you will see a little later.

About 2½km (that's 1½ miles for some of you) along the main avenue you'll come to the Phoenix Monument, perched in the middle of a roundabout. The old bird has been rising from its ashes up there since 1747 and the column was erected by Lord Chesterfield. Have a good gawk about and you'll see a sign pointing to the Phoenix Park Visitor Centre, our next stop.

This is an attraction that has the distinct advantage of being free. And it's well worth a visit. Here you can enjoy an exhibition on the park's history and wildlife, and when you've done that you can relax in the Phoenix Café, which also has a very nifty courtyard area where you can dine alfresco. Adjoining the centre is the fully restored seventeenth-century Ashtown Castle. Interestingly, another building stood on the spot of the castle until 1978. That was being demolished when they discovered the original castle hidden within the walls. Jaysus, they really built their walls thick back then.

Back to the Phoenix Monument and head straight across the road. Over on the right you'll see a big set of gates with a driveway up to them. That's the official residence of the U.S. Ambassador, a stunning eighteenth-century mansion set amid 60 acres of beautiful orchards and gardens. But you're not allowed to see any more than that as you're not important enough. If you would like to be invited to stay as an overnight guest then try and get elected as President of the United States of America, or become Ambassador to Ireland, or marry the ambassador to Ireland. Other than that, your luck's out. Presidents JFK, Nixon and Clinton are among those that have crashed there.

Park trivia

The park is a popular venue for rock concerts, usually held under bucketing rain on a typical Irish summer's day. Previous acts have included Coldplay, Robbie Williams, Duran Duran, Red Hot Chili Peppers and loads of other wrinkly rock stars, as well as lots of youthful ones.

In 1903 the world land speed record was broken on the main avenue in the park when the driver reached the startling speed of 84 mph—the speed limit on public roads at the time was 20 mph.

Winston Churchill lived in a house in the park as a boy and recorded that he had his first coherent memory there—he remembered soldiers carrying out drills when his nanny used to take him for morning walks.

Keep going along that road past the Ambassador's gaff, and, about a hundred metres later, you'll see a large expanse of open land ahead of you, which is known as the Fifteen Acres. The park's herd of wild Fallow Deer are usually to be found loitering happily in this area, looking with bemusement as tourists try to get close for a better snap. The herd of four to five hundred is descended from the original lot introduced back in the seventeenth century.

Here you'll also see the Papal Cross, a 35-metre-high structure made from girders, which one presumes are made from some form of holy steel, and which is set atop a large grassy bank. In winter this sloping bank is one of the most popular places in Dublin for kids to come and slide down the frozen earth. Take a stroll up the steps to the top and gaze out and try to imagine more than one million people—one third of the population of Ireland at the time—who attended mass here when Pope John Paul II visited in 1979. Of course the Irish were very devout Catholics back then. Should the same event occur tomorrow, numbers attending the mass would probably be slightly smaller, like sixty or seventy.

♣ Farmleigh Estate

While you're here in Dublin you're likely to sample the Guinness. Here's your chance to see where all the money has been going that you and the rest of us have been squandering on alcohol for centuries, because the Farmleigh Estate and mansion were originally the home of one of the heirs to the Guinness family. Farmleigh is located to the north west of the park—carrying on along the main avenue past the Phoenix monument, take a left when you come to the crossroads and then the next right. The wealthy spiffs swanked about this beautiful mansion for a couple of centuries before selling the estate and house to the Irish Government in 1999 for about 30 million euro. Magnificent as it is, it was probably worth about a quarter of that at the time, but that's why the Guinness family are rich. The State then spent a further 23 million euro renovating it—work that your local builder, Seamus O'Flaherty & Sons, would have probably done for about fifty grand. But let's not be bitter. The end result is a mansion fit for a queen—in fact Queen Elizabeth II stayed here during her visit to Ireland in 2011. You see, Farmleigh is now the official State Guest House, boasting luxury and splendour inside and out, and is definitely worth a visit, if only so you can stare in envy at the wealth all around you and then reflect on the sad little life you live in your three-bedroom semi-detached gaff with the draughty windows. The grounds are also quite beautiful, featuring a walled garden, a sunken garden, a fountain lawn and lots of nice plants. And on top of all that, entrance is free, so more money left for pints. Details of visiting times below.

DUBLIN ZOO Tel: +353 (0)1 474 8900

Website: dublinzoo.ie

Admission charged.

ÁRAS AN UACHTARÁIN Tel: +353 (0)1 677 0095

Website: www.gov.ie/aras

Tour information: Lo Call: 1890 430 430

PHOENIX PARK VISITOR CENTRE Tel: +353 1 6770095

Website: www.phoenixpark.ie

Admission is free.

FARMLEIGH HOUSE & ESTATE: **Tel:** +353 1 815 5900

Website: www.farmleigh.ie.

Public tours are available Monday–Sunday, including Bank Holidays, from 10am-6pm, provided the house is not in use by some annoying foreign dignitary.

PHOENIX PARK BIKE HIRE: Inside main entrance at Parkgate Street

Tel: 086-26 56 258

Website: www.phoenixparkbikehire.com

Location: Main entrance is 2.5km from the centre of Dublin. If you're going to be walking/cycling around the park, might as well have a rest getting there—we recommend a taxi!

See map on inside back cover.

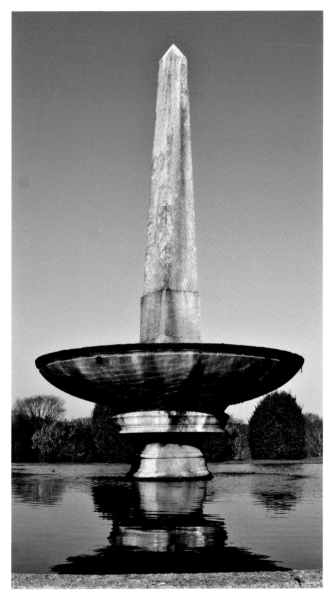

138

⓱ The National War Memorial Gardens

● ●

Other sights nearby: *From Con Colbert Road entrance, Kilmainham Gaol, 750m. Phoenix Park, nearest entrance, 1km.*

Here's the thing, Ireland launched the 1916 Rising against British rule slap bang in the middle of the First World War, and no sooner had it ended than we started the War of Independence, so you'd be forgiven for thinking that we weren't particularly interested in helping Britain slug it out with the Germans in the trenches. Then how come fifty thousand Irishmen died in that war? Well, as they say, it's complicated. But we'll get to that. The War Memorial Gardens were built to commemorate all of those men, and some women, who gave their lives in WW1. And it is one of the finest war memorials in Europe.

♣ The History bit

Here's the background. During WW1, Ireland was still officially British and across the water they were conscripting half the country to replace all the poor souls that were being slaughtered on the battlefields. They then realised they could pack a load of Paddies off to the front as replacement fodder for the German guns, and planned a conscription drive in Ireland. Any eejit could have told them that this would cause a wave of support for nationalists and the cause of an independent Ireland. But there was no telling them, and they drafted a conscription bill. The opposition was so great that they never conscripted a single person here. And yet, almost three hundred thousand people from north and south voluntarily joined up. As you can probably guess, we just don't take kindly to anyone else telling us what to do. However, we'll gladly help our neighbours across the water if it's our idea or if they ask us nicely. The other thing was that many Irish people saw it as a good Catholic thing to do, as small Catholic countries like Belgium had been overrun by Godless hordes, or some such baloney. And then there was the matter of jobs. The Dublin Lock-Out—a five-month strike in Dublin—ended just before WW1 began. Countless families were on the brink of starvation and there were thousands of men out of work. Joining the army was for many the only option if you wanted to make a living. Of course dying isn't much of a living, but that was the chance they had to take.

In 1919 it was decided to build a fitting memorial to those who never came home. Moving with the speed and urgency

for which Irish politicians and public servants have become world-renowned, the War Memorial Gardens were completed in 1939, just in time for WW2. So the official opening didn't happen. Another seven thousand men from the Republic of Ireland died in WW2, despite the fact that we were neutral in the war. When the garden eventually opened officially it would also honour their memory, and all other Irish men and women who served or died in the armies of other nations, including Britain, the U.S., Canada, Australia, New Zealand and South Africa. During the 1970s and 80s the park fell into decline, mainly because some politicians believed that it was a memorial to a British army, and we couldn't be havin' that, now, could we? That claptrap was finally put to bed in the late eighties and the park fully restored and officially dedicated on 10 September 1988, a mere sixty-nine years after it had first been proposed. Well, they do say we Irish never like to rush things.

♣ What's there?

Appropriately for a memorial to men who had died fighting in a British army, a British architect was chosen, and not any oul' geezer, but one of the greatest Britain has produced, Sir Edward Lutyens. Eddie had designed war memorials all over Europe, including the Cenotaph in London, and the Dublin job would be among his finest works. It features a large raised central lawn surrounded by a high granite wall, in the middle of which is the 'War Stone', made of Irish granite, symbolising an altar, which weighs seven and a half tons. (During construction, to increase the number of jobs the project provided, it was decided not to use mechanical equipment, so the War Stone and all the other stuff was manoeuvred into position using pulleys, ropes and Irish muscle!) Either side of this are large fountain basins with obelisks in the centre, and on the slope above this is a cross, and inscribed on the nearby wall are the words: 'To the memory of the 49,400 Irishmen who gave their lives in the Great War, 1914–18'.

At either end of the lawn are two pairs of ornate granite Bookrooms, representing the four provinces of Ireland, which are joined together by pergolas (a fancy word for a shaded walkway, in case you were wondering). Each Book-room contains, that's right, you guessed it, books. These are illuminated volumes containing the names of every one of the

49,400. They used to be open to the public, but because of the threat of damage by vandals/gurriers, you can only see them now by appointment. Beyond these on either side are the gorgeous, tiered, sunken rose gardens, each surrounding a lily pond.

Looking down from the central lawn you'll see a small, domed temple about one hundred metres away, which is the focal point of a series of tree-lined avenues. If you head down there you'll see the gently flowing River Liffey just beyond, which, thanks to a nearby weir, is the favourite haunt of lots of muscular guys and girls rowing up and down in their long pointy boats. With the backdrop of the slope of the gardens to the south and the elevated ground of the Phoenix Park to the north, and the rolling river in between, this is a really pretty, peaceful place to have a picnic, assuming you're not being battered by marble-sized hailstones. But on a fine summer's day it is a popular retreat, although luckily, not too popular as many Dubs favour the nearby Phoenix Park, which means it is always sparsely populated.

If you are planning a picnic, note that there are no shops in the park, so come prepared. In any weather it is a great place for a walk and in fact the riverside walkway continues for two kilometres all the way to the pretty village of Chapelizod in case you're feeling energetic. You will, of course, find a couple of 'refreshment stops' there.

♣ Majestic

Having first visited the Garden of Remembrance to honour the Irish rebels who had been fighting *against* her lot, Queen Liz II then came here to honour the thousands of Irishmen who were fighting *for* her lot. Yes, we do like to complicate things in Ireland. Anyway, the visit to the War Memorial Gardens was another of the highlights of her historic visit, and Lizzie and the then President Mary McAleese laid wreaths at the War Stone to honour the dead.

IRISH NATIONAL WAR MEMORIAL GARDENS, Islandbridge, Dublin 8 **Tel:** +353 1 475 7816 (gardens) **Email:** info@ heritageireland.ie

Admission is free.

Bookroom access: By appointment.

Location: 3.5km from centre of Dublin.

See map on inside back cover. As with any of the sights not in the city centre, the simplest/laziest way is a taxi ride!

⑱ Kilmainham Gaol

• •

Other sights nearby: *National War Memorial Gardens, 750m. Phoenix Park, nearest entrance, 1km.*

No visit to Dublin is complete without spending some time in one of its prisons, though hopefully this will not be because you decided to run down O'Connell Street in the nip or tried to play 'Stairway to Heaven' on Brian Boru's Harp. To be specific, a visit to Kilmainham Gaol is a must for anyone with even the slightest interest in the past, and in particular, Ireland's struggle for independence. Although be warned, there is a good chance you won't emerge through the gates of the prison swapping funny stories about your experience. Yet it is a most rewarding couple of hours.

On one level you can see this as an opportunity to experience what it was like to be banged up in a Victorian prison—prisoners' rights weren't exactly top of the agenda back then. Kilmainham was originally built to house the ordinary criminal, and its architect Sir John Traile would probably have been feckin' mortified that his building would come to be one of the most powerful symbols of Irish nationalism.

♣ The History bit

The gaol takes its name from the area in which it is situated, Kilmainham, which was in the wilds of the countryside when the prison was conceived and built in 1796, at a site known as Gallows Hill. With the hill and tree for stringing up offenders obliterated by the edifice, a new-fangled drop platform was erected on the balcony above the entrance. In the prison's first few decades there was an execution every couple of months. And it was in public, naturally, so the whole family could enjoy a nice Sunday outing, munch a few pigs' trotters and then watch some poor gouger have his neck stretched. And they weren't all murderers and rapists—burglars were commonly sentenced to death by hanging. They didn't mess about back then. Public hangings were eventually banned and executions relocated to a room within the walls.

In its day Kilmainham was considered one of the most advanced prisons in existence:

'(Kilmainham Gaol) . . . for safety, healthfulness, convenience, and compactness is superior to any prison in Europe.'

Or so they boasted. In reality, the early days were pretty squalid, with no segregation for prisoners. Men, women and children were often crammed five to a cell and the prison's youngest inmate was said to have been aged seven. Kids were usually put in prison for stuff like stealing a loaf of bread. And they think they have it rough nowadays when their Mammies won't give them fish fingers and chips for dinner!

As soon as you enter the building you get a sense of the conditions. It is full of narrow, dank and dark corridors and shadowy nooks and crannies. Most of the cells are locked up, but you can peer into the ganky little spaces through spy holes in the doors and imagine a bunch of poor feckers lying about on straw, although it was noted in the early 1800s that many males were supplied with iron bedsteads, while the unfortunate girls were obliged to lie on the flagstones. You will also have the opportunity to enter a cell and have the door slammed behind you, thus catering for the masochistic.

Structurally, the most impressive bit is the East or Victorian Wing, which features a large, barrel-vaulted space with iron galleries and catwalks, lit by a huge skylight. The design afforded the guard a perfect 270-degree view. The amazing acoustics also allowed a guard to hear any hanky-panky in the cells, such as someone ordering out for a pizza. The cells here were designed for solitary confinement, so that prisoners could spend their time reading the Bible and reflecting on their crimes. No doubt much of their reflection was of the nature of 'I'm goin' to beat the livin' shite out of that f***in' judge when I get out of here.'

Imprisoned for freedom

But the real reason Kilmainham is a shrine in Irish consciousness is not because of the run-of-the-mill crooks, but because it also housed, at one time or another, a vast array of major figures from the struggle for Irish freedom, and especially those associated with the 1916 Rising. Hardly had the place opened when it took delivery of the leaders of the 1798 rebellion, quickly followed by those of the rebellions in 1803, 1848, 1867, and 1916, as well as the War of Independence (1919–21) and finally the Civil War (1922–23). The list of inmates reads like a 'Who's who of Irish History':

1803: Michael Dwyer—one of the leaders of the 1798 rebellion, who subsequently mounted a guerrilla war against the crown forces in County Wicklow.

1803: Robert Emmet—leader of the 1803 Rebellion. Hanged, drawn and quartered.

1867: Jeremiah O'Donovan Rossa—legendary Irish Fenian leader.

1881: Charles Stewart Parnell—renowned statesman who led the campaign for Irish land reform and home rule.

1881: Michael Davitt—founder of the Irish National Land League.

1916: Leaders of the Easter Rising. (*See* opposite)

It is interesting to note that class divisions were often evident even in prisons. Charles Stewart Parnell, who was from a terribly posh background, was arrested for his land reform activities. While in Kilmainham he was allowed some of the luxuries to which he was accustomed, and a contemporary drawing shows him sitting in a nice comfy armchair chatting to lady friend in front of a big blazing fire. Such was his stature that the British Government conducted negotiations with him while in prison, resulting in what became known as 'The Kilmainham Treaty', which won major concessions for Irish tenant farmers.

MORE CAVIER MR. PARNELL SIR?

Kilmainham's most famous prisoners were the leaders of the 1916 Easter Rising. In the aftermath of the Rising, courts martial sentenced ninety men to death, most of whom were held at Kilmainham. Fourteen were ultimately executed by firing squad in the Stonebreaker's Yard. The seven signatories of the Proclamation of the Irish Republic—Padraig Pearse, Thomas J. Clarke, Sean Mac Diarmada, Thomas MacDonagh, Eamonn Ceannt, James Connolly and Joseph Plunkett—would subsequently become legendary figures for what many saw as a 'blood sacrifice'. As you'll undoubtedly learn on the tour, Connolly was too badly wounded to stand for his execution so he was strapped into a chair and shot. A striking sculpture representing those executed, complete with bullet holes, stands across the road from the gaol. Up to this point Irish attitudes to British rule had been ambivalent, with sharp division throughout the country. After the executions, the mood of the entire nation shifted towards the nationalists, leaving the British establishment to mutter a collective 'Oops'.

During the War of Independence, hundreds of prisoners were held here, and then, in the Civil War, the Free State Government incarcerated hundreds of anti-Treaty soldiers. It was during this period that a curious incident happened in the gaol. Upon hearing of the death of Michael Collins, who was the republicans' former leader in the War of Independence but who was now their enemy, seven hundred of the prisoners fell to their knees and said a rosary in his honour, such was the reverence in which he was held.

Collins's principal adversary, Éamon de Valera, who would be a major figure in Irish politics for the next five decades and future President of Ireland, was the final prisoner to be held in Kilmainham Gaol. First imprisoned in 1916, he was locked up again during the Civil War, and released in July 1924.

The doors of Kilmainham Gaol finally banged shut for the last time in 1924. Thanks be to Jaysus.

Undying love

One of the most moving experiences of the gaol tour is the account of the last hours of one of the leaders of the Easter Rising, Joseph Plunkett and his fiancée Grace Gifford. Plunkett had proposed to her the year beforehand and Grace, who was a Protestant, decided to convert to Catholicism, which she did in April 1916. She had planned to marry Joseph on the forthcoming Easter Sunday, but had no knowledge of the Rising. When she learned that he was to be executed on 4 May, she rushed into Dublin to buy a wedding ring and then pleaded with the authorities to allow them to marry, to which they acceded. They were married in the tiny Kilmainham Chapel under the watchful eyes of twenty British soldiers with bayonets fixed. Afterwards Plunkett was immediately taken away, although they were granted ten minutes together in his cell later that day, again under the watchful eye of soldiers. Seven hours after his marriage, he was shot. Grace never married again. Grace herself became a prisoner here during the Civil War. A talented artist, she painted on the cell walls, and her Madonna and Child can still be seen.

♣ Constance Markievicz

British visitors may be interested to note the cell of Constance Markievicz, one of the many women who took part in the Easter Rising. After the Rising she was sentenced to death, but this was commuted to life imprisonment because the powers-that-be realised that executing a woman might make the rest of the world think they weren't gentlemen. She was released under an amnesty in 1917 and the following year she was back in her cell, arrested for subversive activities. While in Kilmainham she stood for election and became the first woman to be elected to the British Parliament, but didn't take her seat in protest at British rule in Ireland. That was a shame, really, as you can just imagine the stir

she would have created among those stuffy old farts in the Westminster of the day.

♣ Giving up the ghost

Inevitably, Kilmainham Gaol is a popular visit for ghost-hunters. Given the number of people who've kicked the bucket here, be they brutal axe murderers, people who stole a chicken, patriots or those who just died of some wojus disease, there's bound to be a spirit or two wandering the corridors. Apparently, during the restoration in the 1960s, the principal supervisor lived in the place, and one night noticed that the chapel across the yard was lit up. He investigated, found no one and turned off the lights. When he returned to his quarters he noticed that the lights were on again. He returned and turned them off. This happened three times, leading him to believe that some spectre was behind the phenomenon. Well, either that or a couple of smart-arses who were hiding in a closet breaking their shite laughing.

There were other reports of a painter being blown off his feet and pinned to a wall by a powerful gust of wind—this was in a closed corridor—and also lots of tales of men feeling a ghostly presence pass directly through them, although in all probability this was more likely the chicken curry they'd eaten the night before.

KILMAINHAM GAOL, Inchicore Road, Kilmainham, Dublin 8
Tel: +353 1 453 5984. **Website:** www.heritageireland.ie
Access to Kilmainham Gaol is by guided tour only (**fees charged**). As this is one of the most popular tours in Dublin, it is advisable to arrive early. Only groups of over 10 people may be booked in advance.
Location: The Gaol is 3.5km from centre of Dublin.
See map on inside back cover. The simplest way to get there is to hop in a taxi!

⑲ Croke Park & Croke Park Museum

• •

No, this is not a park with trees and flowers and squirrels and people with fat arses jogging. 'Croker', as it is known by Dubs, is the home of the GAA, (the Gaelic Athletic Association) and Croke Park is a spectacular national stadium and the centrepiece of Ireland's unique sporting heritage.

In case you've just landed from Mars and haven't a clue about Gaelic games, then the main ones are Gaelic Football and Hurling. Other less well-known games are Camogie (ladies' version of hurling) and Handball (like squash, but using your hand instead of a racquet).

But what makes Ireland's national sports quite unique is the vast support they still enjoy in these days of global sports coverage and overpaid nancy-boy soccer stars. Big match final days at Croker attract crowds of eighty thousand, and what many visitors find startling is that the players are ama-

teurs and don't get paid a cent for their efforts. It would serve well the whingeing, big girl's blouses that play for the Real Madrids and the Manchester Uniteds of this world to watch some real men play sport purely for the glory of their team, and not so that they can fart around in a Ferrari with a dumb blonde hanging out the window. If a hurling player were to act

like most soccer players and, every time he got a little tap, roll around on the ground clutching his leg like it had just been bitten by a shark, honestly, his own team mates would probably beat him to death with their hurleys. So welcome to Croke Park. Wimps should best avoid the place.

♣ The History bit

It helps to have a teensy-weensy insight into Croker's background and Gaelic games before you visit the sports cathedral. Gaelic football has origins back in the Middle Ages, while hurling goes so far back that there are references to it in Irish mythology. But it was with the founding of the GAA in 1884 that the sports were first put on an organised basis. And

nowadays there are gansey-loads of local clubs around the country, north and south, with the main national interest in the competitions between the thirty-two counties of Ireland. The first finals in what is now Croke Park took place in 1896, with Tipperary winning in both football and hurling. The stadium was named after Archbishop Thomas Croke, one of the GAA's first patrons, and like the good archbishop, the association had strong links with Irish nationalism, so it was always under the beady, suspicious eyes of the British crown.

When you see the huge, glittering three-tiered arena now, it is hard to imagine that back in 1913 there were just a couple of small, banjaxed stands. After the 1916 Rising, the rubble from the city was piled into a hill at the north eastern end, then terraced over. The section is still known today as 'Hill 16', and it is a favourite place for Dubs fans to mass in their sky blue colours on match days. Croke Park also has another, tragic, link to the struggle for Irish independence: In November

1920, Michael Collins staged a series of assassinations of British intelligence agents in Dublin. In response, British soldiers and the Royal Irish Constabulary entered Croke Park in the middle of a match between Dublin and Tipperary and started indiscriminately firing into the crowd, killing fourteen and wounding hundreds. One of the murdered was the Tipperary team captain, Michael Hogan, and the stand on the western side of the ground was named in his honour.

In the following decades the ground was developed to a capacity of just over eighty thousand—yet somehow in 1961 they managed to squash in the record attendance of over ninety thousand, so a lot of the crowd left the place considerably thinner. In the nineties the entire stadium was redeveloped and the new stadium built in four phases over a decade, without Croker ever closing. The glittering modern new stadium, with a capacity of 82,300, is now the fifth-largest in Europe and arguably the largest amateur sports venue in the world.

One of the unfortunate side effects of the GAA's association with Irish nationalism is that the organisation originally banned its members from playing 'foreign' sports, like soccer, rugby or cricket—or to cut the bullshit, it banned members from playing 'British' sports. This rule was rescinded in 1971, but a ban on the playing of 'foreign' sports at Croke Park continued until as recently as 2005. Many of the old diehards were outraged, but the vast majority of GAA members, players and fans were in favour of ridding the organisation of this claptrap. The GAA allowed soccer

Boo! Boo! Boo!

and rugby internationals to be played in Croker for the first time in 2007, while the national soccer and rugby ground was being rebuilt. Some moronic protestors turned up at the matches waving placards about banning the playing of soccer at Croker, while wearing Celtic FC (soccer) shirts. But all that was forgotten about when, in 2007, Ireland played England in rugby at Croker and the strains of 'God Save the Queen' were heard there for the first time. Unfortunately for England, neither God nor the Queen could save them that day as Ireland hockeyed them 43-13.

The GAA also realised that there were plenty of spondulicks to be had by staging rock concerts at Croker, and the stadium has been host to U2 a few times, Robbie Williams, Elton John, Tina Turner and a whole lot of other megastar head-the-balls.

Scoring at Croker

Croker was truly brought into the modern age when it had its first streaker—some gobshite ran on starkers in the middle of a big game in 2003, but he was quickly caught by the bouncers. Ouch. There have also been several other male streakers since, including one in 2007 when a young plumber darted across the turf in the nip. Later he came on a popular nationwide radio station to tell his story and, hilariously, his Mammy came on another line and 'ate the head off him' on the national airwaves, saying that if he did anything like that again she would 'slap his bare arse for him'. But undoubtedly Croker's best bit of scandal came in 2002, when a young couple broke into the ground at midnight and headed straight for the centre of the pitch for a bit of midfield action. While there they showed the level of passion normally reserved for All Ireland Final days and they both scored repeatedly, before they were tackled by the Gardai, who found them 'in a state of undress'. It was one match at Croker that had a lot of physical contact.

♣ The GAA Museum

Here's your chance to get really stuck into Gaelic games and even to test your own potential as a player (who knows, you might be the next God/Goddess of the GAA world). The museum has been refurbished in recent years and boasts a ginormous collection of trophies, hurleys, jerseys, posters and banners going all the way back to the earliest games, when the players used to sport shorts down to their knees and every person in the crowd wore a hat.

There are videos displaying clips of historic games and a Hall of Fame showing the legends of hurling and football. One thing you should know is that while the players don't get any monetary reward, winning an Ireland medal virtually ensures everlasting glory in your county—all the girls will want to snog you even if your face looks like a cartload of turf. On top of that, GAA fame can open lots of career doors and you'll be getting invitations to open new supermarkets and

swimming pools until you're about ninety-three. The museum also shows the development of the ground from rickety tin shed to super stadium and some of the other famous events that have been held there, such as the 1972 meeting of Muhammed Ali and Al 'Blue' Lewis, or the opening ceremony of the Special Olympics in 2003.

And the other thing you get to do is test your own skills with interactive exhibits—just how well can you give a sliothar (a hurling ball) a decent puck with a hurley. (This will make perfect sense after you've done the tour.)

An entertaining guide also conducts you on a tour of the stadium. You'll get to sit in the VIP seating even if you're a complete nobody and you'll visit the changing rooms where an athletic GAA player with bulging muscles will strip naked before donning his county colours—ha, sorry girls, fooled you, made that last bit up. One of the best bits is to walk down the tunnel into the arena, which you'll do to the accompaniment of a recording of what it actually sounds like on match days. You get to walk pitch-side and later visit the media centre high up in the stand, so you'll get both a worm's and a bird's eye view.

Incidentally, the reason that the stadium is only enclosed on three sides is not that the GAA ran out of dosh or because they lost the plans for the last bit in the pub. It is purely because there are houses and a railway line immediately behind that end and, well, the people living there sort of objected to having bulldozers driving through their living rooms and bedrooms, understandably.

♣ Etihad Skyline tour

Talking of bird's eye view, the Skyline tour is separate to the main tour but well worth forking out the extra cash (it is fairly steep, ha ha, at €25). Only open a couple of years, you get to ascend to the stadium roof and take a stroll around the walkway which gives fantastic views of the entire Dublin skyline, right out as far as Dublin Bay. For those who are a bit wobbly on their feet at such heights, relax, you are always attached to the walkway with a safety harness. And you are accompanied by another entertaining guide who will point out all the interesting bits and bobs to you. There is also a great photo op—part of the platform projects slightly over the pitch. The tour takes about two hours, which includes a safety briefing.

Tip: Bring your binoculars, and unless it is a scorching hot day (in your dreams, pal), bring a jacket.

Whether you think sport is a big pile of crap or not, Croke Park is well worth the visit because it also incorporates history, culture and spectacle. And afterwards, you'll think most over-paid international sports stars really need a kick up the arse. As these things go, Croker's as good as it gets.

CROKE PARK/GAA MUSEUM, Cusack Stand, St. Joseph's Avenue, Croke Park, Dublin 3
Tel: +353 1 819 2323 **Website:** www.crokepark.ie
Admission charged for Museum and Tours.
Location: See map on inside back cover. A bus or suburban train will leave you 500m from the stadium, but to save yourself the hassle, we recommend a comfy taxi ride.

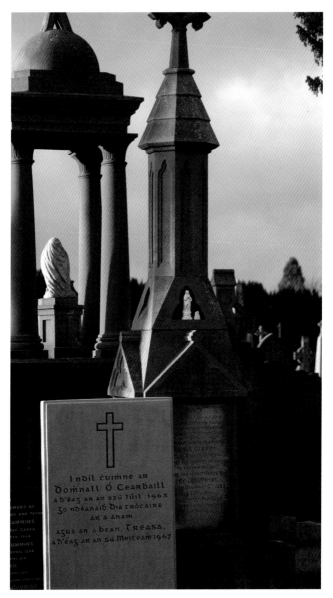

⓴ Glasnevin Cemetery & Museum

• •

Other sights nearby: *From main entrance, 500m to Kavanagh's Pub.*

'I did not come to Dublin to spend my time wandering around a bunch of old graves in a f***ing cemetery!'

Yes, we can just hear the argument when the other half makes the suggestion. As far as you're concerned, the next time you go to a cemetery, you'll be in box. This is a grave error. (Geddit?) Besides being a totally fascinating, moving and completely memorable place to visit, Glasnevin also gives us the opportunity to indulge in some deadly puns. Trust us, people have been dying to get into Glasnevin for nearly two hundred years.

Glasnevin Cemetery's list of residents reads like a who's who of Irish history, political and social. It has some amazing monuments to the famous and not so famous and you could easily bury yourself in the many fascinating stories about the ordinary folk who are pushing up daisies here. The place is a national monument and the brand new museum is really engrossing—it won the European Museum of the Year a couple of years back. It will really bring the entire place to life for you.

♣ The History bit

Back in the early nineteenth century the Catholic Irish had nowhere to bury their dead. As you can imagine, this could cause problems, especially when Grandad Mick started to stink up the place. This was because Ireland's Catholics had just endured over a century of repressive Penal Laws, which originally banned the practice of mass. So Catholics had to be buried in Protestant cemeteries with little or no religious service. Step up Daniel O'Connell, Dan the Man (O'Connell Street, etc.), who won religious freedom for Catholics and used his influence to force the opening of a cemetery for people of all religions. Glasnevin was opened on 21 February 1832. The first burial was eleven-year-old Michael Carey from a poverty-stricken area of inner Dublin.

The cemetery was designed by Patrick Byrne, complete with a high wall and watchtowers, there to deter despicable body snatchers. The guards back then also had a pack of Cuban Bloodhounds, which were originally used to track criminals and runaway slaves.

Since the first burial, over one-and-a-half million people have taken up permanent residency here. Among them lots of really famous ones. But some of the most interesting things you'll learn concern the ordinary people of Dublin and beyond.

Such as the cholera victims who were buried here in the nineteenth century who, from beyond the grave ended up giving cholera to a whole bunch of other people down the road. Or the baby who was killed in crossfire during the

1916 Rising and, as martial law was in effect, had to be buried at 7am with only his grandfather present.

Or the heart-breaking Little Angels' plot, which contains the bodies of fifty thousand babies who were mostly still-born—Glasnevin was the only cemetery in Ireland that would allow the burial of unbaptised babies in consecrated ground.

There are a million other fascinating and moving tales waiting to be dug up. So stop looking like you're going to a funeral.

♣ The Museum

The Glasnevin Museum is a sight to see in itself. A stunning piece of architecture, it includes a visitor centre, crypt museum, restaurant, exhibition space, the Daniel O'Connell lecture hall and also a high-tech genealogy section. So, if you think you've a bit of Irish in you, here's your chance to track down any possible Irish ancestors who have a connection with Glasnevin.

The fanciest gadget in the museum is the ten-metre-long, interactive timeline, which contains the stories of two hundred of the most interesting people buried in Glasnevin. Each individual's story appears on the time-line when they died and can be accessed by touching the surface, so you can read about them and view photos, documents and even film clips.

The City of the Dead is not a Hollywood zombie movie, but an exhibition telling the stories of gravediggers, body snatchers, burial practices and old and new religious beliefs associated with death and burial.

And after the tour, you can have a rest in the fancy new café/restaurant, although hopefully not an eternal one.

♣ Dead Famous

The best way to see Glasnevin is to take one of the guided tours, which are really interesting and not without humour, believe it or not. But in the meantime, here's a sneak preview of some of the more famed inhabitants of the cemetery.

♣ Daniel O'Connell

The largest and most elaborate mausoleum in the cemetery, you'll spot the round tower the moment you arrive. The tower above the crypt is over 50 metres tall and based on the round towers used by Irish monks back in St. Paddy's day. Daniel O'Connell, known as 'The Liberator', was one of the greatest historical figures in Irish history. He died

in Genoa in 1847 while on a pilgrimage and his heart was taken to Rome and the rest of him sent back to Ireland. O'Connell's coffin can be seen and touched through portals cut into the marble surround. Ironically, considering that O'Connell was a pacifist, Loyalist terrorists tried to blow up the tower back in 1971, but the gobshites only succeeded in making a noise loud enough to wake the dead.

♣ Charles Stewart Parnell

'The Uncrowned King of Ireland', as he was known in his day, Parnell was the man who brought about the greatest agrarian transformation in Irish history, returning all the land to us that had been nicked by British colonists. He also brought Ireland to the brink of Home Rule before he was undone by having an affair with another MP's missus, Kitty O'Shea. He was only forty-five when he died of a heart attack. He wanted his grave to be a simple affair and it is—a grass mound marked only by a large boulder taken from his home county, Wicklow. Parnell was a Protestant, but the Catholic clergy didn't show him the respect of attending his funeral because he'd been a naughty boy. Not that anyone else cared—two hundred thousand attended the funeral, so many that it took them until after dark before they all reached the cemetery.

♣ Michael Collins

'The Big Fellow' as he was known, was the man most responsible for Ireland's independence, leading a guerrilla war against the British forces from 1919 to 1921, until the British eventually offered a truce that led to the partition of Ireland. That led to the Irish Civil War during which Collins was tragically assassinated. He was only thirty-one. If you thought Parnell's funeral was well attended, Big Mick's brought half a million people out—almost one-fifth of the population. His grave is a relatively simple one, right behind the cemetery museum. Fresh flowers are a permanent feature.

In 1922, when Collins arrived at Dublin Castle to accept the handover of power, the British leader remarked angrily that Collins was seven minutes late, to which The Big Fellow calmly replied: 'We've been waiting over seven hundred years, you can have the extra seven minutes'.

♣ O'Donovan Rossa

The Fenian leader died in 1915, having spent much of his life in exile in America. His grave is best known as the place where the leader of the 1916 Rising, Padraig Pearse, made his graveside oration, one of the most famous speeches in Irish history. If you happen to be doing a tour at 2.30pm, (Mar–Sept) you'll be lucky enough to catch an actor playing the role of Pearse deliver the famed lines: 'They think that they have pacified Ireland. They think that they have purchased half of us and intimidated the other half. They think that they have foreseen everything: but the fools, the fools, the fools!—they have left us our Fenian dead, and while Ireland holds these graves, Ireland unfree shall never be at peace.' Watch the Irish chests swell with pride . . .

They're just a sampler. Some of the others you'll happen across include famed playwright Brendan Behan, who, like yourself, was partial to a pint or two, or twenty-two. There's also President Éamon de Valera, veteran of the Rising, one of the most influential leaders of Ireland in the twentieth century and Michael Collins' nemesis in the Civil War. Famed fellow Irish rebels who also reside nearby are Harry Boland, Cathal Brugha, Sir Roger Casement and Countess Markievicz, as well as loads more of their comrades. There are a hundred other graves of interest and even some of the graves of people you've never heard of are fascinating—some of them are larger than your house!

GLASNEVIN CEMETERY & MUSEUM, Finglas Road, Glasnevin Dublin 11

Tel: Museum: + 353 01 882 6550

Website: www.glasnevintrust.ie

Entry to the cemetery is free, especially if you're dead, but guided tours or visiting the museum are charged.

Location: Glasnevin Cemetery & Museum is 3km from O'Connell Street.

See map on inside back cover. Simplest way, once again, is a taxi ride.

Dublin Pubs

• •

'Good puzzle would be cross Dublin without finding a pub'.
Thus mused Leopold Bloom, the main character in James
Joyce's *Ulysses*. A few years ago, a computer programmer
called Rory McCann set out to solve the puzzle and
succeeded. His long, weaving route avoided all pubs by
thirty-five metres, so you couldn't pass one on the other side
of the street. Ironically, his route also passed St. James's Gate,
home of the Guinness Brewery. Such is the fame and ubiqui-
tousness of Dublin's pubs that Rory's feat attracted global
news coverage as his achievement seemed akin to charting a
course through New York without meeting any New Yorkers.

Well done, Rory. But the real question is, why would you
feckin' *want* to cross Dublin without finding a pub? Depending
on who you believe or how you look at the map, there are at
least seven hundred pubs in Dublin, and possibly as many as
a thousand. There are all sorts of pubs—big ones, small ones,
old ones, new trendy ones, loud ones, quiet ones. In ninety
percent of these pubs you are guaranteed a *céad míle fáilte*,
a deadly pint, a nice atmosphere and most likely decent food.

The main concentration of good pubs in the city centre is
to be found around the Grafton Street area, along Baggot
Street/Merrion Row and in Temple Bar. Having said that, you
can find decent pubs in almost every street all over the gaff.
The twenty-one pubs listed below—in alphabetical order—
are among the favourites of the authors. They are also shown
on the maps by pint symbols. These represent the sum total
of decades of diligent, passionate and zealous research.
It was a tough job, but someone had to do it.

1 The Auld Dubliner

As you approach from the west along Temple Bar you'll see a beardy old man with a cap and an overcoat, and nearby is his dog, having a piddle against a wall. He's the 'auld Dubliner' of the name. He's a mural. The pub is painted bright red and if you still can't find it, watch for the 'Auld Dubliner' name above the door.

The pub has a fairly ordinary interior, although it does have some pretty stained glass windows. The atmosphere is nice and relaxing by day, rib-crushing by night, but in a fun kind of way. And, hey, you never know who you might be lucky enough to be squashed against. There's a large upstairs bar too. There's live music pretty much all day, mostly of the trad Irish kind, and pretty informal. There's also food available, hearty, good value, mostly of the Irish Lamb Stew variety, but with the occasional Oriental Stir-Fry thrown in.

THE AULD DUBLINER, 24 - 25 Temple Bar, Dublin 2.
Tel: +353 1 677 0527, **Website:** www.thesmithgroup.ie

2 The Bailey

The original pub was famed as a literary haunt, and had in its foyer the door of No. 7 Eccles Street, the fictional home of Leopold Bloom, the main character in Joyce's *Ulysses*. The original interior was gutted in the '90s, but the door was saved and moved to a Joycean museum. Despite the modern décor, some imagine they can still sense the ghostly presence of famed previous patrons, people such as Joyce, Charlie Chaplin, J.P. Donleavy, Patrick Kavanagh, Richard Harris, Peter Ustinov, Evelyn Waugh, John Betjeman, Charles Stewart Parnell and Arthur Griffith, the founder of Sinn Féin. Others just want to get plastered. Brendan Behan was also a regular here, but then Behan was pretty much a regular in half the pubs in Dublin. The décor is trendy, the clientele a mix of the common folk and 'chic' wannabe-arty types, the atmosphere is not as frenetic as some other pubs, the pints are excellent and the food has a distinctly Iberian flavour. There's also a nice seating area outside, and if it's not freezing or pouring, it's a great place to check out passers-by with nice bums.

THE BAILEY, 1-4 Duke St, Dublin 2.
Tel: +353 (0)1 6704939 **Website:** www.baileybarcafe.com

3 The Brazen Head

Supposedly the oldest pub in Ireland, first opening its doors as a coach house in 1198. The present-day pub is from the

eighteenth century, so even that's pretty old. Former patrons tend to be more political than literary, although Joyce, Behan and Jonathan Swift did pop in every now and again for a pint and a ham and cheese toastie. But if you get a sense of rebellion in the air, it's probably the influence of the likes of revolutionaries such as Robert Emmet, Wolfe Tone and Michael Collins, who were regulars. Emmet is still said to pop in occasionally, despite the fact that he was hanged, drawn and quartered by the British in 1803. The pub is said to be haunted by his spirit, so don't say anything derogatory about Ireland! Daniel O'Connell also frequented The Brazen Head, bringing a welcome bit of peace. And you'll find peace there by day, and lots of life by night and a great atmosphere. There is live music every day, a mix of trad Irish and contemporary bands. BTW, Tom Jones performed here just a couple of years ago and Garth Brooks featured the pub in a video. The food is mostly traditional Irish: Bacon and Cabbage, Guinness Stew, etc. Portions are generous, prices reasonable and staff friendly. It's a pretty big pub with several rooms or nooks, large and small, and there's also a good heated patio area for those who want to drink and smoke themselves to death.

THE BRAZEN HEAD, 20 Bridge Street Lower, Dublin 8.
Tel: +353 (0)1 677 9549 / +353 (0)1 679 5186
Website: www.brazenhead.com

4 Bruxelles

Bruxelles has been a pub since 1886, but only in its present incarnation since 1973, when Ireland joined the then EEC, with its HQ in Brussels, or Bruxelles in French. Hence the name. It became a venue for the rock music scene and its most famous patron was probably Phil Lynott of Thin Lizzy, whose life-sized bronze statue stands outside. Some of its other patrons you might have heard of: Oasis, Iron Maiden, Snow Patrol, Paul Weller, Imelda May, Andrew Ridgley, 50 Cent and so on.

There are three bars; the ground level one looks not much different from a traditional Irish pub, although it does double as a sports bar. The other two, the Flanders and the Zodiac,

have more modern, trendy décor and cater for rock music. There is also a heated seating area out front. The food (snacks, lunch or dinner) is reasonably priced and of the traditional, hearty Irish variety, and very tasty at that. None of that foreign muck! The pub is open late on weekdays and even later at the weekend, if you can remain upright that long.

BRUXELLES, 7 Harry Street, Dublin 2.
Tel.+353 (0)1 677 5362
Website: www.bruxelles.ie

5 Davy Byrnes

Back to things Joycean, this pub is one of the most popular stops on Bloomsday, 16 June, when it seems to be hosting an Edwardian fancy dress party, all thanks to it having played a part in *Ulysses*:

He (Leopold Bloom) *entered Davy Byrne's. Moral pub. He doesn't chat. Stands a drink now and then. But in leap year once in four. Cashed a cheque for me once.*

Mr Bloom goes on to order a gorgonzola cheese sandwich, Italian olives, a nice salad and a glass of Burgundy, before Davy Byrne himself makes an appearance:

Davy Byrne came forward from the hindbar in tuckstitched shirtsleeves, cleaning his lips with two wipes of his napkin . . .

Mr Bloom ate his strips of sandwich, fresh clean bread, with relish of disgust, pungent mustard, the feety savour of green cheese. Sips of his wine soothed his palate. Not logwood that. Tastes fuller this weather with the chill off.

Nice quiet bar. Nice piece of wood in that counter. Nicely planed. Like the way it curves there.

You won't find much of that nicely planed counter any more, but it does have a very nice art deco interior. Thanks to the food references in *Ulysses* it has also developed a reputation as a 'Gastropub', i.e., it's got nice grub. The menu is extensive and varied and not unreasonably priced. The pints, and the wine, will definitely 'soothe your palate'. The atmosphere by night is almost enough to inspire one to scale the literary heights.

DAVY BYRNES, 21 Duke St, Dublin 2
Tel: +353 1 677 5217
Website: www.davybyrnes.com

6 Doheny & Nesbitt

A couple of decades back, this was a tiny little bar that was loved by all who could squeeze into it. Because of its proximity to Government Buildings it was popular with prominent politicians who huddled in corners getting pissed and devising devilish plots to get re-elected. There would also be loads of journalists present, earwigging, trying to pick up morsels of secret information for the next day's edition. It's still much the same, although they have extended the original bar out the back into a large lounge, but one that was designed so well it is hard to tell where the old bit ends and the new bit starts. It is a true original Victorian pub and most of the fittings in the interior date from the nineteenth century, as do one or two of the patrons by the looks of them. But they just add to the atmosphere. Young and old flock here. Busy by night and at lunchtime. Food choice is of the traditional fare type, but there is plenty of it, and they do lunch and dinner. Reasonable prices. One of the best pubs in the city.

DOHENY & NESBITT, 5 Baggot Street Lower, Dublin 2
Tel: +353 1 6762945
Website: www.dohenyandnesbitts.ie

Hartigan's

If you're into authentic, you'll love Hartigan's. It's not so much hip, as kip. But in a good way. And it is many people's favourite kip in the world. The seats are worn and tattered, the floor tiles cracked and scruffy, it needs a coat of paint and it's been like that for donkey's years. Perfect. The pints are sensational. The clientele a mix of ordinary Joe Soaps, guys in expensive, pin-striped business suits, office workers and tourists, all combining to create a talky, jocular atmosphere.

If it's food you want, you can make do with a toasted sambo or a pack of Tayto crisps. The smoking area is a concrete yard with a couple of metal tables. All of which sounds like criticism. But it's not. The décor is enlivened by nice stained glass windows, and some of the staining on them is there from the days when punters filled the air with dense clouds of tobacco smoke. The publican, Alfie Mulligan, died, aged ninety, a couple of years back. He was a Dublin institution. But it is still family run. Besides its reputation as a great pub, it also has other claims to fame. It featured in Flann O'Brien's *At Swim Two Birds*. If you're in search of an authentic Dublin pub, you've found it.

HARTIGAN'S, 100 Leeson Street Lower, Dublin 2

Tel: +353 (0)1 676 2280

Website: We don't have any of those new-fangled yokes.

This is not only a very fine drinking establishment, it also hosts a comedy club every night of the week, a club that provided the kick-start for the likes of Des Bishop, Tommy Tiernan, Dylan Moran, Dara O'Briain, Ardal O'Hanlon, Barry Murphy and lots of other funny guys who've since found fame and fortune. But seriously, it is a great, traditional pub with old

ornate wooden bits, very fine pints and for grub there's soup and sambos. Oh, and crisps. The comedy takes place in a small room upstairs and there is music, usually in the basement bar, every night. And they cater for most tastes. Some days it's blues, others jazz, others contemporary bands and on Sunday afternoons trad Irish takes over. You'll have to check the pub's website to see what's happening. The pub is also the starting point for the 1916 Walking Tour of Dublin, and no better place to enjoy a pint before you head off to fight for Ireland's freedom.

THE INTERNATIONAL BAR, 23 Wicklow Street, Dublin 2

Tel: + 353 (0)1 677 9250

Website: www.international-bar.com

9 Kavanagh's
(aka The Gravediggers)

It's not in the city centre, but is here because it is next door to one of the recommended things to see, Glasnevin Cemetery. You might, with the help of that information, be able to figure out where the pub got its nickname. Being right next to a cemetery, naturally it is haunted. And there are plenty of spirits to be found behind the bar. Ha ha. The grave-diggers of old used to pop in here after they'd planted a stiff and apparently there also used to be a serving hatch directly on to the graveyard so they could drink on the job. John Kavanagh opened the place in 1833 and the pub is still owned by the same family. The interior is all old wood panelling with scratched tables and benches, and besides spectral visitors it is frequented by anyone who likes to drink, sit and talk till the cows come home. No TV or blaring music. Pub lovers think they've died and gone to heaven. The pint is first rate and so is the inventive menu, which apparently changes every day. It's mostly Spanish dishes that are raved about. Besides this, Kavanagh's is a one hundred per cent Irish pub experience. No wonder the ghosts keep coming back for more.

KAVANAGH'S, Prospect Square, Glasnevin, Dublin 9
Tel: +353 (0)1 8307978
Location: The pub is hidden in a small, residential square which may be accessed via the Glasnevin Cemetery entrance at the south west corner (during normal opening hours) or via a couple of narrow roads/lanes leading from Botanic Road or Finglas Road— they're used frequently by pedestrians and traffic. **See map.** Alternatively, you can save yourself all that hassle and grab a cab!

 Kehoe's

First off, it is not pronounced *Kee-hoes*. It's more like *Keh-yo*. Sort of. Ah f*** it, never mind. Only Irish people can actually pronounce the name properly. Anyway, Kehoe's is among Dublin's finest, and has been a popular watering hole for over two hundred years. You'll get an idea of the type of pub it is from the fact that the most recent renovation of the downstairs bar took place when the main mode of transport in Dublin was the horse. We're talking nineteenth century here. Kehoe's is all dark mahogany and full of nooks and crannies and secret snugs. There are wooden drawers behind the bar—a century ago they used to hold different types of tea and coffee for sale. God knows what's in them now. There are more bars and rooms to be found upstairs. Actually, the pub is a bit like a mini labyrinth. When you go into the upstairs rooms, don't panic that you've accidentally strolled into someone's living room. It used to be precisely that and when the owner John Kehoe died some years back, it was decided to convert his living quarters into a pub extension—and it really works. On very busy evenings it can look like the pub has the same population as Rio De Janeiro and Beijing put together, and, on fine days, the patronage extends halfway across the street. Yet, like in many pubs in Dublin, the bar staff make all other bartenders on the planet look like a bunch of big girl's blouses. No matter how jammers the place is you'll always get your drink promptly and with a friendly smile. In short, they are GODS. Food is of the ham and cheese sambos variety. But really, who's hungry? Just soak up the atmosphere and the pints.

KEHOES, 9 South Anne's Street, Dublin 2
Tel:+353 (0) 1 6778312 **Website:** www.louisfitzgerald.com/kehoes

🍺 11 The Long Hall

Some people would use the word 'beautiful' to describe an Irish mountain lake veiled with mist at sunrise. Pub lovers would use the word 'beautiful' to describe the Long Hall. It's really quite special as pubs go. It's a kind of Victorian Gin Palace that hasn't changed much in a couple of centuries, except that gin probably isn't the drink most in demand nowadays. It seems to have been carved straight from a single block of mahogany and then fitted with lots of brass and copper, ornate mirrors and antique chandeliers, then decorated with old paintings and antique muskets. It's actually

a listed building. Not to give the impression that this is a musty old place full of equally musty old gougers. The crowd here is a typical Dublin mix of all ages, types, creeds and races, just here to enjoy the craic and the pints. The name gives you a clue to the interior—basically a big long room, and you enter the rear bit under a lovely wooden arch surmounted by an antique clock. The bar staff are friendly and helpful—they seem to work with military precision on busy nights, when despite the crowds, you'll still be able to hear yourself talking. Daytime and weekday nights the Long Hall is a great place for a relaxing pint. Must-see pubs in Dublin? As Irish characters in Hollywood movies say: to be sure, to be sure, to be sure, to be sure . . .

THE LONG HALL, 51 South Great George's St, Dublin 2
Tel: +353 (0)1 4751590

McDaid's

McDaid's was home away from home for the likes of Brendan Behan, Patrick Kavanagh, Flann O'Brien, J.P. Donleavy and Liam O'Flaherty. Due to the frequency of his visits here, it was once suggested to Behan that he was a writer with a drinking problem—he responded that no, he was a drinker with a writing problem. Brendan came from a fervent Republican family and he and his father were under the constant scrutiny of the Garda Special Branch. His Ma was always complaining to his Da that the back garden was overgrown with weeds and needed to be dug. So the Da made an anonymous call to the Gardai and told them that the IRA had buried a secret cache of guns in the Behans' back garden. Within hours a horde of Special Branch were fervently and fruitlessly digging up the Behans' garden. Problem solved.

If you feel any ghostly presence while here, it might be explained by the fact that McDaid's was once the Dublin City Morgue. It was also once converted into a church for the

Moravian Brethren, whoever they are. (Apologies to all Moravians reading this book.) Their presence explains the stained glass and the tall Gothic windows. After they left, and the building became a pub, there was some continuity in that people flocked here to drink religiously. Another regular in the fifties was Nobel Prize–winning physicist Erwin Schrödinger, who you might have encountered in Merrion Square. He used to spout on here about his theories on Wave Mechanics, and the locals would nod away with apparent interest, although Erwin might just as well have been talking Swahili. McDaid's still has the sort of atmosphere that encourages such varied banter. It's not a huge pub, and is busy at weekends, like everywhere in Dublin. But never mind that. Squash your way in and breathe in the ambience.

MCDAID'S, 3 Harry Street, Dublin 2
Tel: +353 (0)1 6794395

Mulligan's

If it was good enough for JFK, it's good enough for you. Yep, the U.S. President used to drink here. Don't believe it? Well, ok, it's only partly true. JFK did drink here, but he wasn't the President at the time. He was working as a journalist for Hearst Newspapers when he was just a slip of youth back in the early fifties and Mulligan's was one of his favoured drinking spots.

It was also the location of a scene in Joyce's *Dubliners*, when a bunch of guys arrived here to finish off the pub crawl they'd been on. And no better place. It has been serving pints for centuries and the interior still looks the part. Mulligan's has always had an eclectic clientele—it is close to the Liffey so attracted hordes of thirsty dockers, rubbing shoulders with actors and theatre luvvies from the nearby, beautiful Theatre Royal, which was tragically demolished in the sixties. The walls of one part of the pub are covered with posters from those theatre days. It was also popular with journalists—the defunct *Irish Press* was close by, and one or two of the nearby *Irish Times* hacks are still known to sneak in here for a sip of sherry, or eight pints of Guinness. Students from Trinity College complete the mix of regulars. It is another of those pubs with hidden nooks and crannies and lots of old mahogany. It is the perfect place to exchange a bit of gossip while sipping a perfect pint. Like most popular Dublin pubs, by day it is a haven of tranquillity and calm, by night it is hit by a tidal wave of chatter. Much like any other decent pub in Dublin.

MULLIGAN'S, 8 Poolbeg Street, Dublin 2
Tel:+353 (0) 1 6775582 **Website:** mulligans.ie

14 Neary's

Neary's was originally owned and run by the Honorary Consul to Guatemala. Not a word of a lie. His name was Leo Neary and he bought the pub in the nineteenth century. Between trips to Central America he managed to create a pub with a fine reputation, an attractive interior and exterior and a lovely pint. You can identify the place by the two arms protruding

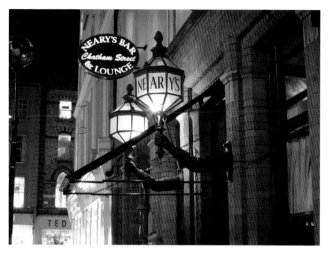

from the doorway wall supporting a couple of fancy lanterns. Inside it has quite a Parisian feel, with a pinky-grey marble counter top and brass fittings. It is quite an elegant gaff. There's also a little snug-type area which is very popular. There's another bar upstairs called The Chatham Lounge, which was refurbished a while back, and has a nice oval bar. This is another place for socialising in the manner of the more genteel Victorians, and please note there's no singing allowed, in case you have the urge to burst into a drunken version of 'Goodbye Muirsheen Durkin'. The pub backs on to the Gaiety Theatre, which has traditionally made it a big hit with actors and theatre luvvies. Among the customers who have sampled Neary's delights in recent years are Colin Farrell, Glenn Close, Will Ferrell, Cillian Murphy, Gabriel Byrne and many others of the Hollywood glitterati.

Of course the pint here is first rate, as are the sambos, which seem to have more packed in between the bread slices than is possible according to laws of the physical universe. They're fairly pricey, but you get what ye pays for, as the man says. Neary's is a relaxing haven most days and weekday nights but can be fairly hectic as Dubs let their hair down at the weekend. Still, even then it has quite a refined air about it.

NEARY'S, 1 Chatham St, Dublin 2
Tel: +353 (0) 1 677 8596

15 O'Donoghue's

Possibly the most famous pub in Dublin, O'Donoghue's has been jigging along to the beat of Irish music for the best part of a century. This is the kind of place where musicians just drop by, whip out their instruments and strike up a tune. Tin whistles, flutes, fiddles, accordions, bodhrans, guitars, uileann pipes and all other sorts of yokes you've probably never heard of belt away in harmony. There's lots of foot-tapping, and every now and then someone caught up in the fervour of the jig or the reel impulsively shouts *'Yeooow!'* or something similar. Countless Irish folk legends have started their careers here, most famously The Dubliners, Christy Moore and the Fureys. Such is its reputation that the likes of Bruce Springsteen and Billy Connolly have popped in for a pint and a tune. The pub itself is all old wooden partitions, many of which look like they're going to collapse at any moment, but don't worry, they've looked that way for yonks. This is a really popular spot for musical Dubs and tourists. Every now and then a tour group is disgorged into the relatively small bar and you can temporarily feel the walls bulging like an over-inflated balloon. But don't let that turn you off. There's also a very large covered and heated smoking area in a laneway outside if it gets too packed inside. Actually it holds more people than the pub itself. For food there's the tasty toasty ham or the cheese sambo. Music, grub, drink, atmosphere, laughter, chat—at O'Donoghue's, you can forget about the big bad world outside.

O'DONOGHUE'S, 15 Merrion Row, Dublin 2
Tel: +353 (0) 1 6607194 **Website:** odonoghues.ie

 16 O'Neill's

When you enter O'Neill's you first have the impression of a nice little old pub. Then you go in a bit and there's another bigger bit and then you go round the corner and there's another narrower bit. And there are bits within the bits, sectioned off by wooden partitions. And then there's the upstairs bit. And then there's the upstairs upstairs bit for smokers. When it's busy, it's easy enough to get a bit lost. But every bit is brilliant. Dark panelled wooden walls, cosily lit corners, big mahogany drinks displays, old signs advertising ancient whiskeys and cigarettes, the pub is endlessly interesting. There's been a pub in some form on this spot for three centuries, and it has existed as O'Neill's since 1927. Being close to Trinity it has always attracted its share of studenty-types. But it has also attracted every other type of Dub, and occasionally they all seem to arrive at the same time. Being so large, there is almost always a seat to be located in some nook or other. And the choice of booze and food is equally brilliant. There are over forty draft beers on offer, including craft beers. The food is as tasty as Scarlett Johansson and served cafeteria-style. It is mostly of the Irish traditional sort but as good as it gets, and you can happily indulge in the classic Irish snack of Guinness and oysters here. Also, the portions are large enough to feed a hippopotamus. There is live trad Irish music every night, and an impressive smoking area upstairs, complete with glass roof and retractable canopy.

But anywhere in O'Neill's will leave you with a warm glow inside. Especially if you've just downed several Irish whiskeys.

O'NEILL'S, 2 Suffolk Street, Dublin 2
Tel: +353 (0) 1 679-3656 **Website:** www.oneillsbar.com

The Oval Bar

Although it originally opened in 1820, the wonderful Oval was a casualty of the 1916 Rising, it being at the centre of the action, just a stone's (or a hand grenade's) throw from O'Connell Street. And unfortunately the interior was gutted. Happily, the curved Victorian frontage survived and the inside was lovingly restored the following year—and it pretty much looks the same today as back in 1917. It has a lovely authentic feel—customers and décor alike—and there's a nice relaxed atmosphere about the place. The staff are friendly and helpful and there is a reasonably priced menu, mostly Irish recipes. (The Guinness stew is said to be legendary!) But eating is only your tertiary concern in The Oval. Your secondary concern is drinking. Your primary concern is talking, laughing and having the craic. And there's plenty to be had in this, one of Dublin's most loved city centre pubs.

THE OVAL BAR, 78 Middle Abbey Street, Dublin 1
Tel: 01 872 1264
Website: www.theovalbar.com

The Palace Bar

Although lots of the pubs in the Temple Bar area were founded back in the nineteenth century, only a few splinters of the original pubs remain and many of them have been rebuilt, expanded, extended, refurbished and often banjaxed to cater for a bigger/younger gang. Possibly the only truly authentic pub in Temple Bar is right on its fringe—just at the start of Fleet Street at the Westmoreland Street boundary of the area. It is called The Palace, and appropriately, the friendly staff treat their customers like royalty. Décor-wise little has changed since it opened its doors in 1823, from its wood and glass exterior to its beautifully ornate interior, the long bar sectioned off by partitions so you can gossip away to your heart's content in private. The pub opens into a broader, square room towards the back, which is lit by a big skylight, and which often resounds to the beat of trad music. The Palace has plenty of literary connections, it having been a regular watering hole for the likes of Patrick Kavanagh, George Bernard Shaw, Brendan Behan and Flann O'Brien, and for decades it was the haunt of countless journalists from the nearby *Irish Times*. The pub is the perfect escape from the normal frenetic atmosphere of Temple Bar—come into the Palace and relax the bod, soak up the atmosphere, and of course, soak up the perfect pints on offer.

THE PALACE BAR, 21 Fleet Street, Temple Bar, Dublin 2
Tel: (+353) 1 671 7388
Website: www.thepalacebardublin.com

🍺19 The Stag's Head

Guess how it gets its name? Yes, there is a big stag's head over the bar. And there are stags' heads pictured in the stained glass. And there's a famous mosaic of a stag's head on the ground outside. Enough stag. This competes with several other Dublin pubs as the best-preserved Victorian gaff in the city. Deep mahogany walls interspersed with colourful windows, mahogany panelled ceiling, chandeliers, brass fittings, Connemara marble counters, antique bits all over the place. The pub opened its doors in 1870 and has been opening them to happy customers every day since. It is hidden away down a little back street, and finding it by chance is like discovering oil in your back garden. You can find it by walking down a tiny covered passageway on Dame Street, heading away from Trinity, about forty metres from the turn off for South Great George's Street. Or you can reach it via another narrow road leading off Exchequer Street. Oh, just look at the map. It was the first pub in Ireland to have electricity and the place generates an electric buzz of its own at weekends when there is live trad music. There's also a decent menu of Irish food at reasonable prices. It is jammers come Friday or Saturday, although you'll almost always find a seat earlier in the day or on weeknights. The clientele are a mix of Dubs and people like yourself. You'll be very welcome in the Stag's Head, another of Dublin's most revered pubs.

THE STAG'S HEAD, 1 Dame Court, Dublin 2
Tel: +353 (0) 1 6793687
Website: www.louisfitzgerald.com/stagshead

The original pub was established in 1840 when the population of Dublin was about a quarter of a million, which is roughly the same number of people who seem to cram into The Temple Bar pub on weekend nights. Having said that, if you don't mind spending your evening like a sardine, it's actually got a great atmosphere, lots of live trad music and friendly bar staff. During the day or weekday evenings it is a much more civilised place to sip a pint or two and you'll actually have a chance of parking your bum on a seat. Some find the prices here a bit steep, but they're comparable to most of the pubs in the Temple Bar area. They serve a decent menu, slightly more adventurous than your average Irish traditional fare, although they offer some of that as well. When you enter via the main door it appears to be a small, cosy Dublin bar. Walk on through and discover an expanse of bustling rooms—

and there's also a big, heated smoking area/beer garden that actually appears to be part of the pub interior. A couple of years ago in The Temple Bar, a musician called Dave Browne entered the *Guinness Book of Records* for the longest continuous guitar playing session—114 hours and 20 minutes!

THE TEMPLE BAR, 48 Temple Bar, Dublin 2
Tel: +353 (0) 1 6725287
Website: thetemplebarpub.com

Toner's

Last stop on our pub crawl through Dublin's finest establishments. And a great place to start or finish any pub crawl! It is forty shades of brown—the wood, the nicotine staining from smoking inside in days gone by, old scratched wooden benches smoothed by a million Irish arses. It opened in 1842 and was taken over by Mr James Toner in 1923, when he operated it as a pub and a grocery store—handy excuse for a pint if the wife sent out for a packet of biscuits and some tea. The drawers that held the groceries are still behind the bar and there's a little 'museum bar' displaying some of the bits and pieces from back in the day. It has a small, though famous literary connection—and it's not Joyce or Behan for once. Genius he may have been, but W.B. Yeats never appreciated the merits of Ireland's pub culture. His fellow writer, Oliver St John Gogarty, brought him to Toner's in the twenties and bought him a sherry, which he dutifully sipped, then turned to his companion and said: 'Fine. I have seen a pub. Now, will you kindly take me home.' Presumably he then arose and went to Inishfree. (That's a literary joke, just in case you've never read any of Yeats's poems.) There's also a movie connection—a scene from the Sergio Leone western 'A Fistful of Dynamite', starring James Coburn, was shot here in 1971.

Food is a toastie sambo and a bag of crisps. There is also a patio area in case it is warm and sunny (ha ha) or if you want to have a smoke. This is large enough to accommodate the population of the Greater New York Metropolitan Area. In fact, it was large enough to accommodate a performance by Mumford & Sons a couple of years back. Toner's is a classic original Dublin pub with a classic pint and a classic atmosphere.

Now, here we are, twenty-one pubs later. Surely you've had enough. Well, ok, seeing as we're in Toner's, just one more for the road. Ok, well, maybe one or two . . . or three . . .

TONER'S, 139 Baggot Street Lower, Dublin 2
Tel: +353 (0) 1 6763090
Website: tonerspub.ie

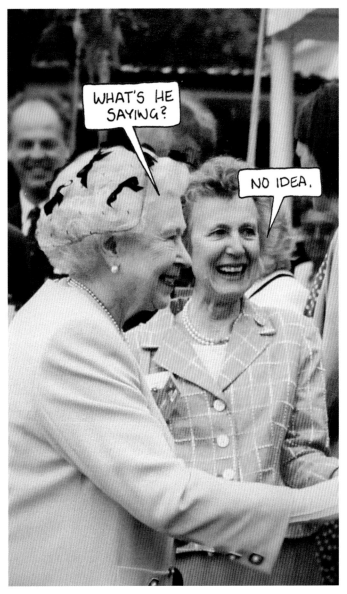

Dublin Slang Guide

- -

In case you have trouble understanding the occasional phrase or word used in this book, here is a brief dictionary of Dublin slang terms you'll find in the text.

Act the maggot (v)	Engage in tomfoolery.
Ate the head off (expr)	To criticise harshly.
Banged up (expr)	Put in prison.
Banjaxed (adj)	Damaged beyond repair/ Very tired.
Bejaysus (expr)	The life, as in 'frightened the life/ bejaysus out of me.'
Blather (n)	Bullshit.
Bollox (n)	Testicles.
Bowsie (n)	Disreputable character. Good-for-nothing.
Brutal (adj)	Awful, hideous.
Cailín (n)	Not really slang, but the Irish word for 'girl'.
Céad míle fáilte (expr)	Again not slang, but Irish for 'a hundred thousand welcomes'.
Craic (n)	(Pronounced 'crack') Fun, enjoyable social interaction, chatter, laughter, drinking.
Crap (n) (v)	Faeces/To have a bowel movement.

Cute hoor (n)	Resourceful person of dubious character.
Da (n)	Father.
Deadly (adj)	Great, brilliant.
Dosh (n)	Money.
Dosser (n)	Lazy person or good-for-nothing.
Dub (n)	Dubliner.
Eejit (n)	Naïve or stupid person, often used light-heartedly.
Fair play to you (expr)	Well done! Good man!
Fecker (n)	Person.
Feckin' (adj)	Polite, socially acceptable version of the 'f' word.
Fluthered (adj)	Very drunk.
Gaff (n)	House or place.
Ganky (adj)	Disgusting, repulsive.
Gansey-load (expr)	A great many.
Gawk (n) (v)	A look/To look at.
Gazillion (n)	A very large number.
Geebag (n)	Person, esp. a woman, of unpleasant character.
Gee-eyed (adj)	Really, really drunk.
Get hockeyed (expr)	Be beaten comprehensively, esp. in sport.
Ginormous (adj)	Really, really big.
Gobdaw (n)	Person of very low IQ.
Gobshite (n)	Stupid, unpleasant person.

Gouger (n)	Sly, repulsive person.
Have the shite kicked out of you (expr)	To be severely beaten up.
Head-the-ball (n)	Any person whose name you don't know.
In the nip (expr)	Nude.
Jacks (n)	The toilet.
Jammy (adj)	Lucky.
Kip (n)	Horrible place.
Like a mad yoke (expr)	Insanely angry.
Ma (n)	Mother.
Make a bollox of (expr)	Do something incompetently.
Make a hames of (expr)	Make a complete mess of.
Mammy (n)	Mother.
Manky (adj)	Really dirty.
Mortified (adj)	Very embarrassed or horrified.
Mot (n)	Girl, girlfriend.
On the lash (expr)	On a drinking session.
Oul' (adj)	Old.
Piss Artist (n)	Someone who is frequently drunk.
Pissed (adj)	Drunk.
Rat-arsed (adj)	Really, really, drunk.
Shite (n)	Crap, faeces.
Slag (v)	To verbally abuse in a jovial manner.
Slapper (n)	Woman of low morals and poor taste.

Sleeveen (n)	Devious, repulsive person.
Spondulicks (n)	Bank notes/Money.
Starkers (adj)	Naked.
Wagon (n)	Unpleasant or unattractive woman.
Wojus (adj)	Utterly useless, awful, horrible.
Yoke (n)	Any object, or a derogatory reference to a person.
Yonks (n)	A very long time.

For a complete guide to Irish slang, check out the best-selling and hilarious *Book of Feckin' Irish Slang* and the *2nd Book of Feckin' Irish Slang* by Colin Murphy & Donal O'Dea.

Photograph credits and acknowledgements:

Cover credits: Beer glass © Julian Rovagnati/Shutterstock;
clover © serazetdinov/Shutterstock

Images clockwise right to left: © cmfotoworks/Depositphotos; © jovannig/
Depositphotos; © jovannig/Depositphotos; © Rob Wilson/Shutterstock;
© jvanderwolf/Depositphotos; © arturdebat1984/Depositphotos,
© Hob Spillane/Shutterstock; © Lauren Orr/Shutterstock

Many thanks to RinzeWind for the image of the Guinness Storehouse,
page 40, Finbarr Connolly at museum.ie for the Ardagh Chalice, page 74,
Emma Byrne for Kilmainham Chapel, page 151, Kilmainham Gaol Collection
for Countess Markievicz, page 152, Simon Fitzpatrick, Leinsterman, for Croke
Park, page 154, Shane Collins for the overhead view of Croke Park, page 161,
Liam Hughes for Glasnevin Cemetery, page 168, Karen Roe for the Queen,
page 200.

A very special thanks to infomatique's William Murphy for the following
images: the Hapenny Bridge, page 96, O'Connell Street, page 108, the *Jeanie
Johnston*, page 114, the Gate Theatre, page 124, the Phoenix Park, pages 126
& 131, the War Memorial Gardens, pages 138 & 142, Glasnevin Cemetery,
pages 162, 164 & 166 and Mulligan's, page 187. This guy knows the streets of
Dublin like the back of his hand. To get a real feel for the soul of Dublin, his
site **www.streetsofdublin.com** is genuinely well worth a visit.

If you enjoyed this book, you'll love the Feckin'
collection from Colin Murphy and Donal O'Dea:

The Feckin' Book of Irish Slang

The Feckin' Book of Irish Sayings

The Feckin' Book of Irish Sex and Love

The 2nd Feckin' Book of Irish Slang

The Feckin' Book of Irish Recipes

The Feckin' Book of Irish Songs

The Feckin' Book of Irish Quotations

The Feckin' Book of Irish Insults

The Feckin' Book of Irish Trivia

What Are We Feckin' Like?

The Feckin' Book of Everything Irish

The Feckin' Book of Irish History

Now That's What I Call A Big Feckin' Irish Book